Family W
in The Cotswolds

Gordon Ottewell

HIGH INTEREST · LOW MILEAGE

Scarthin Books, Cromford
Derbyshire
1997

A

Family Walks Series

General Editor: Norman Taylor

THE COUNTRY CODE

Guard against all risk of fire
Fasten all gates
Keep dogs under proper control
Keep to paths across farmland
Avoid damaging fences, hedges and walls
Leave no litter
Safeguard water supplies
Protect wildlife, plants and trees
Go carefully on country roads
Respect the life of the countryside

Published 1986. Revised 1989. Partially revised 1993. Revised 1995. Revised 1997

Phototypesetting, printing by Higham Press Ltd., Shirland, Derbyshire

Illustrations and photographs all by the author.

Maps by Ivan Sendall

Cover photograph Lower Slaughter (Route 7).
Courtesy of Gloucestershire County Council

ISBN 0 907758 15 0

Ford Over Windrush, Kineton

Preface

'Unless you go slowly you will never see England at all'.

These words, written by S.P.B. Mais in his book 'England's Pleasance', the first book on the countryside that I ever read, remain as true now as when they were written, over half a century ago.

Years after first reading them, their memory was rekindled for me when, as I led a party of children along a country lane on a school field-study trip, one of them exclaimed 'I wish we could go on like this for ever!'

I warmed to the sentiment, and still do. Most children, given the opportunity, enjoy the countryside. The love and respect gained in childhood remains with them for the rest of their lives, to enrich and sustain in a complex, demanding world.

Walking families are happy families - good walking!

Acknowledgements

I must thank George Power, of Scarthin Books, for suggesting that I write this book and for all his invaluable assistance in the task, always willingly and patiently given.

I am deeply indebted too, to my wife, who not only took the photographs, but also typed the manuscript and encouraged me throughout.G.O.

About the author

A native of Derbyshire, Gordon Ottewell has lived in the Cotswolds for over 30 years. He contributes a monthly 'Wold Walk' feature to 'Cotswold Life' magazine.

His other books on the Cotswolds include:

Wildlife Walks in the North Cotswolds: Thornhill Press.

A Cotswold Quiz Book: Barn Owl Books.

Gloucestershire - A County Quiz Book: Barn Owl Books.

Warde Fowler's Countryside: Severn House.

A Cotswold Country Diary: Barn Owl Books.

Theme Walks in Gloucestershire: Thornhill Press.

Gloucestershire Countryside: Minton & Minton.

Cotswold Villages: Sigma Press.

Contents

Map of the area

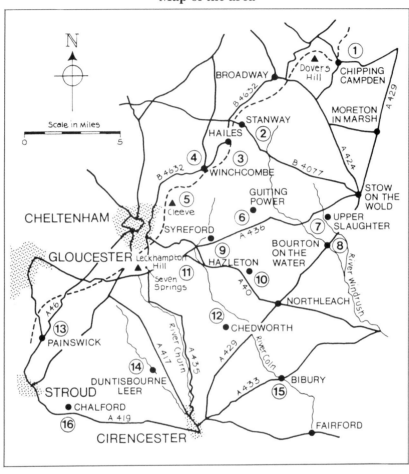

N

Scale in Miles

0   5

BROADWAY

Dovers Hill

① CHIPPING CAMPDEN

MORETON IN MARSH

STANWAY

HAILES ②

④

③

WINCHCOMBE

GUITING POWER

STOW ON THE WOLD

CHELTENHAM

⑤ Cleeve

SYREFORD

⑥

UPPER ⑦ SLAUGHTER

GLOUCESTER Leckhampton Hill

⑨

HAZLETON

BOURTON ON THE WATER

⑧

⑪

Seven Springs

⑩

NORTHLEACH

⑫

CHEDWORTH

⑬ PAINSWICK

River Churn

⑭

DUNTISBOURNE LEER

BIBURY

STROUD

⑮

CHALFORD

A 419

FAIRFORD

⑯

CIRENCESTER

4

Introduction

There are many books on walking in the Cotswolds, as a glance at the shelves in any bookshop will reveal. This is hardly surprising, for the region provides a unique blend of varied scenery, attractive villages and congenial walking conditions, guaranteed to delight anyone prepared to make the effort to discover the region in the only true way - on foot.

This book differs from the others in that it is intended as a gentle introduction to walking in the Cotswolds with the family very much in mind. Although by no means exclusive to families, the routes are planned with interests and stamina of children at heart. They tend therefore, to be comparatively short, with a pub or teashop situated roughly midway along the route wherever possible. Cotswold gradients are unlikely to present many problems to young walkers, especially as the walks generally end with an easy stretch of downhill walking. Although some road walking is necessary on a few of the walks, this has been kept to an absolute minimum. The walks, which vary between 1½ and 8 miles, are without exception circular, with retracing of steps involved on only two of the routes.

In walking, as with all other activities, children are at their happiest when interested and involved. Under the heading 'Attractions', mention is made of a few of the features along each route which may appeal to children. Some of these, such as grassy hollows or fording places, offer the chance for play; others, such as the names of birds or wild flowers likely to be seen along the route, are intended to stimulate interest and provide enrichment generally. Enterprising parents - and children too - will find many other attractions to absorb them during the course of the walks.

Choosing a walk

Unless the children taking part are seasoned walkers, it is advisable to choose one or two of the easier walks first. Children whose only experience of walking is to the nearest shops or park will find a long spell of walking along uneven and sometimes muddy footpaths hard going. In the case of very young children, it may be best to walk part of the route to begin with; even then, it may be necessary to turn back! A good idea is to make contingency plans so that if the party gets half way, and the little ones are on the point of rebellion, rescue can be arranged by meeting motorised friends at the pub en route, or by an adult hurrying back to collect the transport.

To assist with the choosing of routes, they are grouped under headings according to difficulty at the back of the book.

Allowing sufficient time

Each walk is intended as the best part of a day's outing, allowing time for play, exploration and rest stops. It is better to over-estimate rather than underestimate the time required; thus avoiding the need to have to 'route march' the latter part of the journey. As a rough guide, allow a pace of around a mile per hour for very young children, graduating to two miles per hour for the experienced ten-year-old.

What to wear

British weather being what it is, it is best to go prepared for the worst! Even on a dry day there is always the chance that a youngster will end up soaked if the walk follows a river or crosses a ford. For the grown-ups, traditional hiking boots are best, though any comfortable, waterproof shoes with a good grip will do. Children quickly grow out of expensive walking boots, so trainer-type shoes with wellington boots as a back-up are adequate. Waterproof outer clothes are essential for every member of the party - never rely on it not to rain! A spare sweater for the youngsters is advisable, and a complete change of clothing is a must for the more accident-prone little ones. If the walks are being attempted in the colder months, make sure that the children are very well wrapped up to begin with; a child loses heat more rapidly that the average healthy adult.

Conditions underfoot
It should be remembered that during and after prolonged wet spells, footpaths can be extremely muddy and slippery. It is sometimes possible to make a slight detour to avoid badly affected places but often there is no such alternative. This should be borne in mind when planning expeditions.

Public rights of way
All the walks included in this guide follow public rights of way. In most cases, the path is signposted and well worn and therefore easy to follow. Occasionally however, because of infrequent use, the route may not be evident. Crops may obscure its course, or in extreme cases, a path may have been temporarily obliterated by ploughing. If in doubt, walk round the edge of the field to regain the footpath further on, avoiding damage to walls and fences.

The maps
With the exception of that relating to Route 10, Wold Villages, all maps are drawn to a scale of 2½ inches: a mile. In combination with the route descriptions, they are sufficiently detailed to be used without reference to any other maps. Nevertheless, many walkers will wish to take the standard Ordnance Survey sheets with them, and the numbers and grid references of the appropriate sheets are given with each route.

Refreshments
Most of the pubs en route allow children accompanied by adults into their premises. Many also have beer-gardens, while others are situated near a village green or similar open places. In the few cases where children are not allowed inside, the pubs are mentioned nevertheless, since their locations are sufficiently pleasant to drink and relax outside if the weather is good.

If packed lunches are carried, remember that most licensees do not approve of such food being consumed on the premises. Closing times should be borne in mind, especially on Sundays. Aim to arrive at the pub before 2.00 p.m. weekdays and 1.00 p.m. on Sundays, if you are buying lunch, since catering often ceases well before closing time.

Teashop opening times vary according to the time of year and expected custom, but most can be relied upon to stay open until five or six o'clock during the summer months.

Transport to the area
Although it is assumed that most people will travel to the area by car, the starts of some of the walks can be reached by bus. In some others it is possible to start and finish at another point along the walk, where there is a bus stop. Brief details are given at the end of the route descriptions and there is a list of bus operators at the back of the book.

Map Key

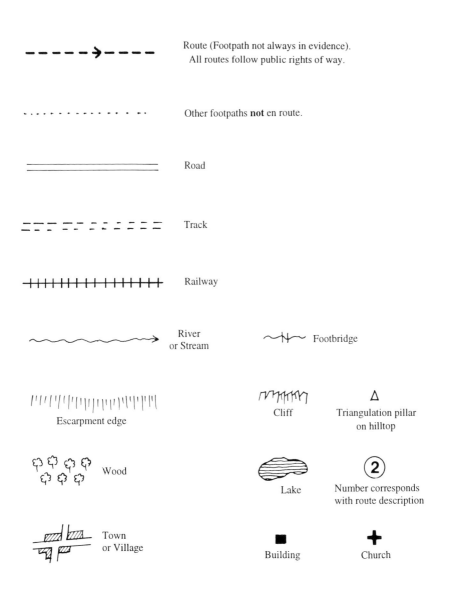

Route (Footpath not always in evidence). All routes follow public rights of way.

Other footpaths **not** en route.

Road

Track

Railway

River or Stream

Footbridge

Escarpment edge

Cliff

Triangulation pillar on hilltop

Wood

Lake

Number corresponds with route description

Town or Village

Building

Church

Water mill, Lower Slaughter (Route 7)

Around Chipping Campden

Walk 1

Outline

Chipping Campden - Dover's Hill - Chipping Campden.

Summary

This short walk follows the route of the Cotswold Way up to the top of the scarp overlooking the Vale of Evesham. The views from here are impressive, as indicated by the presence of an Ordnance Survey triangulation pillar and a topograph.

Attractions

Dover's Hill, the destination of this short walk, is the most northerly eminence of the Cotswold escarpment. It was once called Campden Hill and sweeps in a curve, creating a natural amphitheatre. It was renamed Dover's Hill after Robert Dover, a local gentleman who started his own Olympic Games here early in the 16th century. An artist's impression of Dover, wearing a feathered hat and riding a white horse, can be seen on the National Trust collection box in the car park. Many of the so-called games were tests of strength of the most violent kind - shin-kicking, singlestick fighting, wrestling - as well as hare-coursing, cock-fighting and horse-racing. The Puritans banned the games but they were later revived and continued until the nearby land was enclosed for agriculture. The hill was saved from would-be developers earlier this century and was later presented to the National Trust.

Walk 2

Outline

Chipping Campden - Broad Campden - Chipping Campden.

Summary

This is a pleasant, easy country walk, included for the benefit of those families who wish to tackle a second on-foot rural excursion after sampling the delights of the town. The last stage of the walk involves retracing steps.

Attraction

Broad Campden is a picture-postcard village, tucked away to the south of Chipping Campden and accessible only along minor roads and footpaths. The village has a long association with the Quaker movement and the Friends' Meeting House, which was built in 1663, is perhaps the oldest in the country. Earlier in this century, several well-known craftsmen settled in the area, one of whom, C. R. Ashbee, converted a derelict Norman Chapel into a house, which can still be seen. Hulls' House, next to the church, was the home of Jonathan Hulls, who invented the first steamboat in 1737.

continued on page 12

9

Route 1

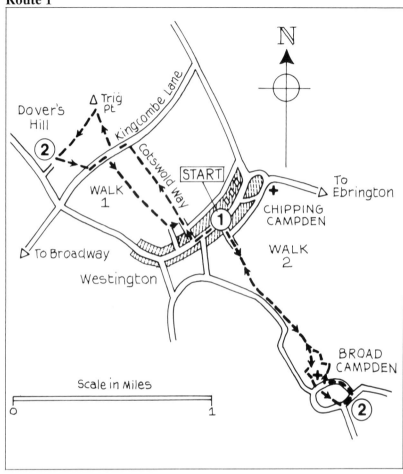

Route 1

Around Chipping Campden

4½ miles
(two separate walks - 2 and 2½ miles)

Start

Chipping Campden. The town lies on the B4035, 12 miles south of Stratford-on-Avon and 2 miles north of the A44 (A424) Evesham-Stow road. Ample street parking is available along High Street, on which stands the Market Hall, from which both these short walks commence. (O.S. Sheet Landranger 151, G.R. 153393).

Walk 1 (To Dover's Hill & return). 2 miles.
Route

1. *From the Market Hall facing across the road, turn right along High Street and right again by the Catholic Church for Hoo Lane. Follow the Cotswold Way signs up the lane, which soon becomes a bridleway. Turn left on reaching Kingcombe Lane (beware traffic) and in a short distance turn right along a signposted footpath by a hedge side for Dover's Hill. The hill is reached over a stile. Bear left along the edge, passing a trig. point to reach a topograph near the car park.*

2. *To return to Chipping Campden, follow the footpath from the car park entrance back to Kingcombe Lane. Turn left, then right along a footpath signposted to Chipping Campden, which crosses a field before dipping to meet a hedge on the left with the town visible ahead. Cross a stile in this hedge and then two more on the right-hand edge of an orchard. The route passes new houses before following a footpath to the left along the back of some houses to meet a road. Cross diagonally to the left between gardens and turn left at the bottom to reach Hoo Lane once more. Turn right and retrace your steps to the town centre.*

Walk 2 (To Broad Campden & return). 2½ miles.
Route

1. *From the Market Hall, cross High Street and pass through the archway of the Noel Arms and over the inn yard to a road. After passing a school, the road narrows, passes a recreation ground and meets a road. At the junction, follow a signposted footpath to Broad Campden to the left, parallel to the road and separated from it by a hedge. Soon the path diverges from the road and climbs to a fork by a stone slab. Take the right fork and go through a kissing-gate and into the grounds of a large house. (Maidenwell). Follow the footpath signs by the house and through another kissing-gate. The route continues along a walled path to meet a road opposite a Quaker Meeting House. Turn right into Broad Campden and after passing the church, cross a road to follow a narrow footpath between fences. Cross a stream and climb to a road.*

2. *Turn left and soon, left again along a lane signposted 'Unsuitable for Motors.' Back at the church, turn right, passing Hull's House, and keep straight on until a footpath branches off on the left just before Quaker Cottage. This path links up with the outward route by the entrance to Maidenwell. Turn right to retrace steps back to Chipping Campden.*

11

Attractions in Chipping Campden

Few if any, small English towns can compare with this place, either for beauty of form or for a sense of historical tradition. The church is a treasure-house, containing among other intriguing features, a memorial brass to William Grevel, the foremost wool merchant of the 14th century, said to be the largest brass in the county. There are also life-size alabaster effigies of Sir Baptist Hicks and his wife, who were so rich that they lent money to King James I. The gatehouse to their long-since demolished mansion can still be seen, together with the market hall that they gave to the town. The Woolstapler's Museum is well worth a visit. Do not miss the memorial garden dedicated to the plant collector, 'Chinese' Wilson, a native of the town.

Refreshments

There are plenty of cafes and inns in Chipping Campden.

The Cricket Pavilion on Staddle Stones, Stanway

Stanway and Stanton

Outline

Stanway - Stanton - Shenberrow Hill - Lidcombe Wood - Stanway

Summary

Stanway and Stanton are widely recognised as two of the loveliest of the Cotswold villages. Unlike Broadway and Bourton-on-the-Water, their appeal is based solely on their historical and architectural associations; those seeking gift shops and gimmickry will leave empty-handed. From Stanway, the route crosses a fine stretch of parkland before skirting fields at the approach to Stanton, where it passes along the village street, climbing steadily, and continues as a rough track past the houses up towards the summit of Shenberrow Hill. Beyond some old quarries, a ridge walk (part of the Cotswold Way) heads southwards towards Shenberrow Farm, sited within a prehistoric camp. From here, the route descends to Stanway through Lidcombe Wood.

Attractions

Stanway may be small but there is plenty to see. The bronze war memorial at the crossroads depicts St. George slaying the dragon. At the entrance to the village stands a striking gatehouse dating from about 1630. Stanway House itself is of Tudor origin but has been largely rebuilt. Beyond St. Peter's church, a glimpse can be had of the fine tithe barn, standing in private grounds. This was built in the 14th century and has been so well preserved that it is still used for village functions. Finally do not miss seeing the cricket pavilion, opposite the start of the footpath to Stanton. This stands on staddle stones, in the manner of a haystack in bygone times, and was given to the village by Sir James Barrie, the creator of Peter Pan.

    Stanway Park contains a fine collection of trees: oak, horse chestnut, beech, including the copper variety, and cedar. Bird life, in consequence, is quite varied, and keen spotters should be able to identify woodpigeon, stock dove, jackdaw, rook, magpie and possibly jay among the larger birds, and several members of the tit tribe.

    Stanton is more compact than Stanway and it is hard to realise that it had fallen on hard times when it was bought by the architect Sir Philip Stott in 1906. Today its beauty seems almost too good to be true. Many of the houses have datestones - several from the 17th century and one of 1577.

    Shenberrow Hill rises to almost 1000 feet and the climb offers splendid views of Bredon Hill and the other Cotswold outliers, as well as of the lowland landscape beyond. Shenberrow Farm lies within an Iron Age hill fort, covering 4½ acres, and among the finds excavated here were a bronze bracelet, an iron knife, and two bone needles.

    The downward path through Lidcombe Wood can be a little difficult after rain, so care is needed. A good range of woodland plants can be seen but the bird life is harder to spot than in the open parkland passed through earlier. The thumping sound heard on this section of the walk is made by an hydraulic ram pump, one of several in the locality bringing water up the valley to hilltop farms.

Route 2

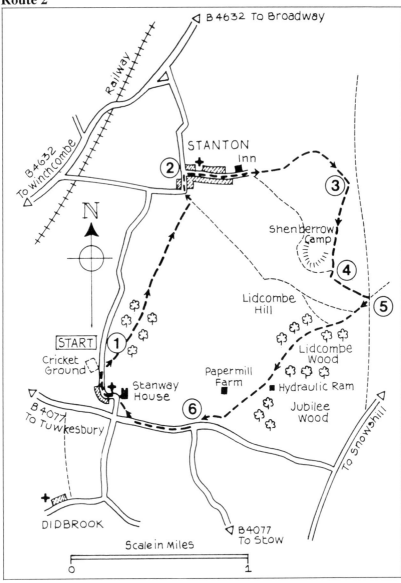

B 4632 To Broadway

Railway

B 4632 To Winchcombe

STANTON Inn

② ✚

③

N

Shenberrow Camp

④

Lidcombe Hill

⑤

START

①

Cricket Ground

🌳🌳🌳

Lidcombe Wood

🌳🌳🌳

Stanway House

Papermill Farm

Hydraulic Ram

Jubilee Wood

⑥

To Snowshill

B 4077 To Tewkesbury

✚

DIDBROOK

B 4077 To Stow

Scale in Miles

0   1

14

Route 2

Stanway and Stanton   5 miles

Start

Stanway village. It lies just north of the B4077 (Tewkesbury-Stow road), a mile east of its junction with the B4632 (A46) (O.S. Sheet Landranger 150, G.R. 060322). Park on the verge on the edge of the village.

Route

1. *After seeing the village, walk along the Stanton road and take the footpath signposted 'Stanton 2 km. Cotswold Way', into the park opposite the cricket field. Marker posts indicate the way. Beyond the park, a clear footpath leads to Stanton.*

2. *Bear right in the village and follow the main street, ignoring any side turns, as far as the Mount Inn. Just beyond the inn, follow the signposted footpath climbing between hedges. As it rises higher, this path passes through rough pasture with fine views behind.*

3. *Eventually, after a long steady climb, turn right over a cattle grid at a crossroads of tracks to follow the Cotswold Way to Shenberrow Farm.*

4. *Just before reaching the farm, turn left through a gateway to follow a signposted bridleway, which passes between the farm buildings. At the point when the farmhouse comes into view on the right, turn left. The bridleway climbs to reach a T-junction with another track.*

5. *On reaching the junction, turn right and immediately right again to cross a field diagonally. Keep on to cross a second field to reach a signboard erected by Stanway Estates. Ignore a stile on the right into the woods. Instead, follow the blue arrow sign, descending the track to the right to enter Lidcombe Wood. From now on, the route is indicated both by green estate marker posts and by official blue arrows.*

6. *Leave the wood by a farm and continue to meet the road. This is the B4077. Descend the hill along the pavement to a Cotswold Way signpost on the right, which leads back to Stanway.*

Access by bus

Castleways buses from Cheltenham and Tewkesbury (limited service).

Refreshments

The Mount Inn, Stanton. Morning coffee. Lunches. Garden. Children welcome.
The Old Bakehouse, Stanway. Teas.

Hailes Abbey Ruins

Hailes Abbey and Winchcombe

Outline
Hailes Abbey - The Pilgrim's Way - Winchcombe - Fluke's Hill - Salter's Lane - Hailes Abbey

Summary
From Hailes, this route follows the Cotswold Way long-distance footpath over fields and along a meandering lane to Winchcombe. From the town, the route crosses the little River Isbourne and climbs through more fields by Stancombe Wood before crossing a stretch of wild country with fine views to reach the ancient Salt Way. From here, a steady descent along the little-used Salter's Lane back to Hailes completes the walk.

Attractions
Hailes, with its abbey and church, now a tourist attraction, was for centuries a place of pilgrimage. The Cistercian abbey was founded in 1246 and was famed for its sacred relic, said to be a phial of Christ's blood, which was later found to be honey, coloured with the flowers of saffron! The ruins, although scanty are still impressive, and there is a small museum. The church is even older than the abbey, and contains some 700-year-old wall paintings depicting fantastic monsters and hunting scenes.

The lane linking the Hailes footpath with Winchcombe is known by two names, the Pilgrim's Way and Puck Pit Lane. The latter stems from the early English words for goblins' hollows and it needs but little imagination to sense shadowy forms lurking behind the bushes along the ancient track!

Winchcombe also had its abbey, although no trace of it remains. It was much older than that of Hailes, having been built in 788 by the Mercian king Kenulf. Here, the attraction for pilgrims was the shrine to the boy king Kenelm, son of Kenulf, who according to legend, was murdered by his tutor on the orders of his scheming sister. The legend is a strange and bloodthirsty one which, although discredited by historians, is kept alive by two stone coffins, one large, the other small, said to have been those of Kenulf and Kenelm, which can still be seen in Winchcombe church.

Another reminder of the part the lost abbey played in the history of Winchcombe can be found at the junction of High Street and North Street. The former George Inn, which stands here, was built before the abbey was destroyed and provided accommodation for the many pilgrims visiting the shrine of King Kenelm, who had been made a saint. The gallery once used by the pilgrims can still be seen, together with a doorway bearing the initials RK, standing for Richard Kydderminster, abbot of the abbey at the time.

The return route from Winchcombe to Hailes provides something of a challenge, climbing above Stancombe Wood to the oddly-named Fluke's Hill, from where there are excellent views westward. Leaving the gorse and scrub behind, the walk ends with a downhill stretch of road walking to meet the Cotswold Way once more, not far from the abbey ruins.

Refreshments
There are several inns and cafes in Winchcombe.

17

Route 3

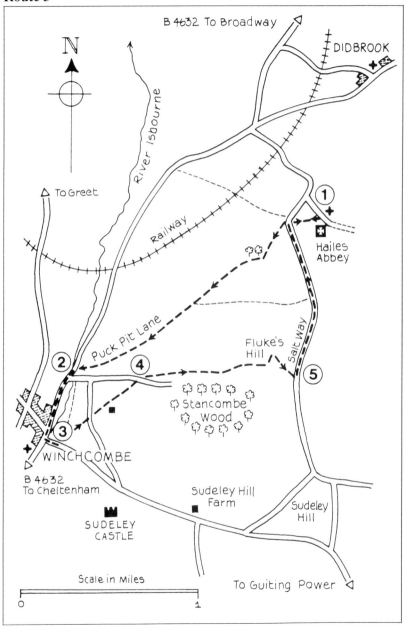

B 4632 To Broadway

N

DIDBROOK

River Isbourne

To Greet

Railway

① Hailes Abbey

②

④

Puck Pit Lane

Fluke's Hill

Salt Way

⑤

Stancombe Wood

③

WINCHCOMBE

B 4632 To Cheltenham

Sudeley Hill Farm

Sudeley Hill

SUDELEY CASTLE

Scale in Miles

0   1

To Guiting Power

Route 3

Hailes Abbey and Winchcombe   5 miles

Start

Hailes Abbey car park. Hailes is 1 mile east of the B4632, 2 miles N.E. of Winchcombe, and 2 miles S. of the Toddington roundabout (where the A438 and B4077 meet the B4632, formerly A46). O.S. Sheet Landranger 150, G.R. 050300.

Route

1. *Cross the road from the car park and pass through a gate signposted 'Winchcombe 3 km. Cotswold Way'. The route is marked by arrows and white circles all the way to Winchcombe. Make for a gate to the right of houses ahead. Pass through and follow a drive to a road. Turn right and soon left through a gateway and along a track as far as two venerable old oaks, where the footpath goes off to the right. It then crosses two fields half left (white discs indicating its course) and after a kissing gate, half right towards a distant power-line post. Through the next kissing gate the path rises to reveal Winchcombe ahead. Soon, it dips to cross a bridge and descends a sloping field to join Puck Pit Lane (The Pilgrim's Way).*

2. *At the foot of this lane, turn left along the B4632 (beware of traffic) and over the River Isbourne into Winchcombe.*

3. *Leave the town by turning left down Castle Street. Cross the bridge and in 50 metres turn left up a narrow alley between two Cottages. Pass through a kissing gate and cross a field diagonally to the right to another kissing gate in a hollow leading to a road. Turn left and in 50 metres right over a stile into another field with a farm ahead. Aim for the left-hand corner of the farm. Cross a stile and a corner of the farmyard and go through a gate. Climb the slope to a junction of fences. Bear left here by a huge oak and through a gate into a lane.*

4. *Follow the signposted footpath opposite over a stile and climb through the bramble patches ahead, crossing two stiles. Continue the climb, with woods ahead and to the right, aiming for a gap between the two. The ascent, through scrub, is steep and the actual path vague. The marker posts with their yellow arrows should be watched for. Beyond the scrub, pass through a handgate and turn left to follow the field boundary as far as a sharp left-hand corner with dense scrub and bracken ahead. Here, instead of continuing along the boundary, go half-left up an ill-defined path and over a stile in a wire fence. Keep straight on through the scrub to a marker post at the top of the slope. Ignore a handgate straight ahead; instead, follow the arrow to the left into a clump of trees. Leave the clump over a stile by a stone wall and after descending a bank over another stile, go through a gate in the wall on the right. Cross the field along a course parallel to the wood on the right, crossing a stile to reach a road through a gate.*

5. *Turn left along this road and descend to the junction of the Cotswold Way footpath walked earlier, turning right by a cottage back to Hailes Abbey.*

Corner Cupboard Inn, Winchcombe

Winchcombe and Belas Knap Long Barrow

Outline
Winchcombe - Belas Knap - Humblebee - Wadfield - Sudeley Park -Winchcombe.

Summary
Beginning and ending at the little Saxon town of Winchcombe, this walk climbs the Cotswold scarp to Belas Knap, a spot rich in prehistorical associations and offering fine views on a clear day. A short stretch of road walking is followed by an easy descent, passing Humblebee cottages and the remains of the nearby Roman villa to Sudeley Park along a footpath and so back to Winchcombe.

Attractions
A Royal seat with its own county for a short while in Saxon times, Winchcombe may have lost its status but its charm remains. There was a fine abbey here (See Route 3) until the reign of Henry VIII, whose widow, Katherine Parr, lies buried in the nearby chapel at Sudeley. In the 17th century, the cultivation of tobacco brought some prosperity to the town, but the government, anxious to protect the trade in Virginia, sent soldiers to Winchcombe to destroy the crop.

Visitors are fascinated by the grotesque gargoyles arranged round the walls of St. Peter's church. They were supposed to frighten away the devil but the modern generation may well find them more amusing than fearsome. The stocks, too, are somewhat out of the ordinary. Situated at the junction of High Street and North Street, outside the museum, they have seven holes, one of which is said to have been provided to hold a one-legged ne'er-do-well who lived in the town. Another odd sight is the name 'Treacle Mary' on a house in North Street. This name refers to an old lady who once kept a sweetshop here, and who specialised in making treacle toffee. The Corner Cupboard Inn on Gloucester Street is said to be haunted by the ghost of a young girl while Rabbit Box House across the road contains stonework taken from the destroyed abbey.

Belas Knap long barrow is a prehistoric burial mound some 5,000 years old. As the notice nearby explains, it has been excavated at various times recently, mostly in the 1920's, after which the entire earthwork, including the fine false portal, was carefully restored. Altogether, the remains of over 30 people were unearthed during these excavations, including five children, together with animal bones, pottery and flint flakes. Some of the skeletons appear to have been from later periods. The absence of other remains, such as ornaments, suggests that grave robbers had entered the barrow many years before.

The wooded hillside known as Humblebee How has no connection with the familiar insect; instead, its name is said to be derived from ancient words describing a scarred hillside. More interesting perhaps is the origin of the name of the handsome 18th-century farmhouse of Wadfield. This was once woadfield, so called from the plant grown locally to produce blue dye used in the Cotswold wool trade.

continued on page 24

Route 4

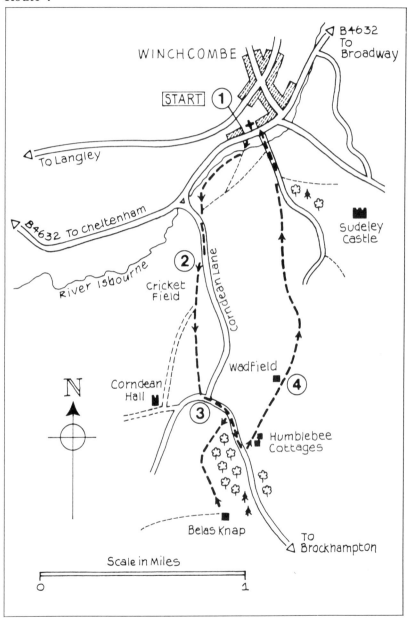

WINCHCOMBE

B4632 To Broadway

START (1)

To Langley

B4632 To Cheltenham

River Isbourne

Sudeley Castle

(2)

Cricket Field

Corndean Lane

N

Corndean Hall

Wadfield

(4)

(3)

Humblebee Cottages

Belas Knap

To Brockhampton

Scale in Miles

0   1

Route 4

Winchcombe and Belas Knap Long Barrow   5 miles

Start

Winchcombe, 7 miles N.E. of Cheltenham, on the B4632 (formerly the A46 - Broadway and Stratford road). The town has two car parks. The walk starts at Queen's Square, alongside the B4632, almost opposite the church. (O.S. Sheet Landranger 163, G.R. 023282).

Route

1. *In Queen's Square, take the footpath between the fine Jacobean house and the Chandos Almshouses. At the foot of this lane, turn left, then right along a path with a 'No cycling' sign to the recreation ground. Turn right to follow the River Isbourne, passing through a gateway and keeping by the river round a left turn to a kissing-gate. Reach Corndean Lane by aiming just to the right of a double power pole. Cross a stile and turn left along the lane.*

2. *In about 400 metres, turn right along a track signposted 'Public footpath Belas Knap'. After passing a cricket field, leave the track over a stile on the left and climb a large irregular field, following the waymarks to reach a junction of two roads over a stile.*

3. *Follow the signpost the short distance to the footpath up to Belas Knap. This ¾ mile section of the walk is so well signposted - and well-worn - that it will be omitted, and the remainder of the route follows: Reaching the road once more from the Knap, turn right and proceed (warily, because of traffic) for another 500 or so metres before turning left along the Cotswold Way by Humblebee Cottages.*

4. *Skirt Wadfield Farm to the right and cross a stile just beyond the farmhouse by the side of a gate. With a hedge on the right, descend through two fields (with Sudeley Castle slightly to the right ahead) and after following the side of a small wood, cross a stile in the hedge on the right. Turn left and with the hedge on the left keep on to cross a footbridge. Winchcombe church tower is now almost in line with the path ahead. Cross another small bridge and stile near a power pole. The path now veers to the right. At the next bridge and stile, the path heads half-right over old ridge-and-furrow, passing a telephone pole to reach a road. Turn left and follow the road into Winchcombe.*

Access by bus

Castleways buses connect Winchcombe with Cheltenham and Broadway.

Sudeley, once an ancient settlement, is now merely a few scattered farms grouped around the splendid castle. This, together with the church in which Katherine Parr lies

Sudeley, once an ancient settlement, is now merely a few scattered farms grouped around the splendid castle. This, together with the church in which Katherine Parr lies buried, can be visited. There is plenty to see - tapestries, paintings, collections of toys and dolls - and an adventure playground that cannot fail to summon up fresh reserves of energy into supposedly tired limbs.

Refreshments
There are both cafes and inns in Winchcombe.

Castle Rock,

Cleeve Common

High Cotswold - Cleeve Common

Outline
Cleeve Common masts - Cleeve Cloud - The Ring - Cleeve Hill (optional) - The Washpool - Cleeve Common masts.

Summary
As the title of this walk suggests, its route traverses the highest part of the Cotswolds and, at a little over 1,000 feet above sea level, offers the closest comparison with mountain walking to be found anywhere in the region. Apart from an optional diversion for refreshments to Cleeve Hill (a roadside straggle of houses and inns surprisingly part of Woodmancote parish), the walk comprises footpaths throughout, the greater part being along the Cotswold Way, and therefore well marked. As befits hill walking, the gradients are fairly steep in places, but the only real hazard comes from balls on the municipal golf course!

Attractions
Fresh breezes, fine views and springy, sheep-nibbled turf provide sufficient appeal to lure thousands to Cleeve Common every year. The regulars swing clubs, exercise dogs, climb rockfaces, fly kites and model aircraft or stroll along favoured paths, while visitors stride out purposefully along the Cotswold Way. Yet despite all this activity, the Common retains its distinctive quality of space and freedom and offers, for those who seek it, plenty of natural and ancient history.

As its name implies, the Common, an area of more than 3 square miles, is common grazing land and owing to its unique value as wildlife habitat is scheduled as a Site of Special Scientific Interest. Because of the mixture of underlying rocks, Cleeve Common is partly natural limestone grassland, rich in lime-loving flowers and the insects on which they feed, and partly moorland, covered with gorse and heather, the last remaining expanse of such habitat in the Cotswolds. Little wonder that botanists have recorded several hundred different plants here, many of which, such as some of the orchids, are extremely rare. Bird life, however, apart from skylarks and meadow pipits, is limited.

The history of the Common makes a fascinating story. Early men built a hill fort, the remains of which are passed on the walk, and also an earthwork known as the Ring, which contained a hut settlement in prehistoric times. Later, the Common was extensively quarried, and the sites of this activity, together with the scree and unused rock, can still be seen. Sheep have always played an important role in the life of the Common, and the Washpool, together with the keyhole-shaped sheep-dip at the foot of what is appropriately known as Watery Bottom, are passed on the walk. It is in this well-watered locality that many of the Common's rarest and most beautiful wild flowers can be found but should on no account be picked.

Route 5

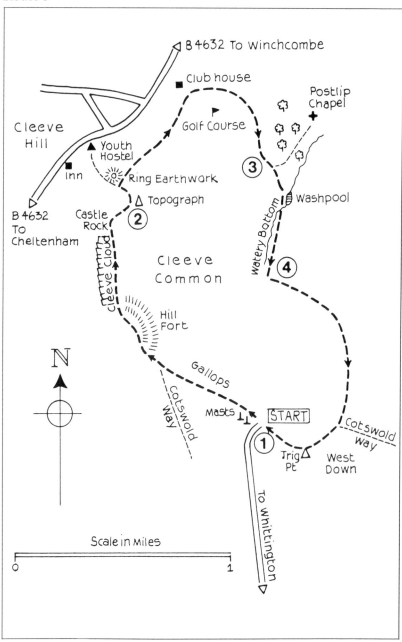

B 4632 To Winchcombe

Club house

Postlip
Chapel

Golf Course

Cleeve
Hill

Youth
Hostel

Ring Earthwork

Inn

Topograph

Washpool

③

B 4632
To
Cheltenham

Castle
Rock

②

Cleeve
Common

Watery Bottom

④

Cleeve Cloud

Hill
Fort

N

Gallops

Cotswold
Way

Masts

START

Cotswold
Way

①

Trig
Pt

West
Down

To Whittington

Scale in Miles

0   1

26

Route 5

High Cotswold – Cleeve Common   4½ miles

Start

The radio masts on Cleeve Common (O.S. Sheet Landranger 163, G.R. 994248). The approach is best made from Whittington, a village ¼ mile north of the A40, 4 miles east of Cheltenham and a mile from Andoversford. Turn left at a T-junction in the village and follow winding lanes for about 3 miles. Park by the wall near the gate on to the Common.

Route

1. Turn left through the gate in the direction of the signpost 'Cleeve Hill 2m'. Walk along the edge and in about ⅓ mile pass a stile on the left, followed soon afterwards by a Cleeve Common notice board. The route is indicated for the greater part of the way by Cotswold Way marker posts - white posts with yellow arrows and white dots on a black background. From the second of these posts, climb via a golf course to reach a triangulation pillar and a topograph at 1040 feet above sea level.

2. Descend from this point as indicated by the marker posts. Part way down the slope, (those wishing to obtain lunch at Cleeve Hill should make a diversion here by descending along the footpath indicating Youth Hostel,) turn right to pass above the Ring earthwork in the direction of the golf clubhouse. Pass an old quarry on the right and before reaching the clubhouse, branch off to the right at another marker post to pass along the rim of another quarry (used as a car park) on the left. Winchcombe and Sudeley Castle now come into view ahead. Keep to the edge of the gorse (and beware of golf balls!). Soon the track veers to the right and the masts appear in the distance straight ahead. The route now dips steeply to a valley bottom.

3. At the foot of the slope, turn right along a track, ignoring a tempting stile into woodland on the left. Pass the washpool and pond and continue up the valley as far as a marker post pointing up a steep slope on the left.

4. Eventually, after a stiff climb, the route levels out, passing through heather and gorse. Just beyond a right-hand bend, bringing the masts into view once more ahead, leave the Cotswold Way at a marker post pointing left. Instead, keep straight on along the grassy track back to the masts, making a slight diversion, if so desired, to the triangulation pillar by the Common Wall (at 1083 feet above sea level, the highest point in the Cotswolds).

Refreshments

The Rising Sun, Cleeve Hill. Morning coffee. Bar lunches.
The High Roost, Cleeve Hill. Morning coffee. Garden Lunches. Garden. Children welcome.

Dragonfly

Musk Orchid

Yellowish-green. June-July.

Upper Windrush Valley

Outline
Guiting Power - Castlett Farm - Pump Bottom - Guiting Power.

Summary
This is a pleasant, easy-paced walk through some of the mixed open and well-wooded country that typifies the upper Windrush valley. From the village of Guiting Power, the walk follows one of the main tributary valleys along the fringe of Guiting Wood. After leaving the woodland, the route crosses a fine stretch of wold landscape to the tiny village of Kineton, from which the final stage of the walk crosses farmland to rejoin the first stage near Castlett Farm.

Attractions
As befits a walk along an unspoiled river valley, water - and the plants and animals attracted to it - provides the chief source of interest. Kineton may be tiny, but it boasts three fords (two on the Windrush and the other on its tributary), and all three lie on the route. The first encountered, that associated with the tributary stream, is crossed by cars at intervals, so care must be taken.

The other fords, in the village, are comparatively little used, one has a delightful clapper-style bridge alongside, which is almost as popular with young children as the fords themselves.

Water-loving plants abound in the vicinity of the fords. Blue brooklime and water forget-me-not, pink willow herb, and forests of horsetail, a primitive plant related to the vast fleshy trees which gave rise to coal seams, can all be found nearby.

Animal life is harder to spot, but can be discovered with a little effort. By patiently turning over the wet stones, such aquatic creatures as freshwater shrimps and caddis fly larvae are revealed. Among the birds, watch out for the dainty pied wagtail and its beautiful relation, the grey wagtail, which appears occasionally along these clear little streams.

By contrast, the woodlands and grassy verges offer their own range of wild flowers and birds, together with a host of butterflies on sunny summer days. The purple heads of bellflower are sure to catch the eye, as is pink restharrow, so called because its wiry roots made ploughing difficult, and fragrant marjoram, well-loved by insects. Watch out for yellowhammers along the lanes and for blue and great tits and woodpeckers in the woods.

Guiting Power is a good example of a thriving, well-maintained Cotswold village with its own resident landowner. The honey-coloured limestone of the buildings, which include shop, post office, two inns and a centre for environmental education, is quarried locally. The church has Norman origins.

The Cotswold Farm Park
2½ miles NE, is open daily between May and September, and contains a comprehensive collection of rare breeds of farm animals. Plenty of interest for all the family.

Route 6

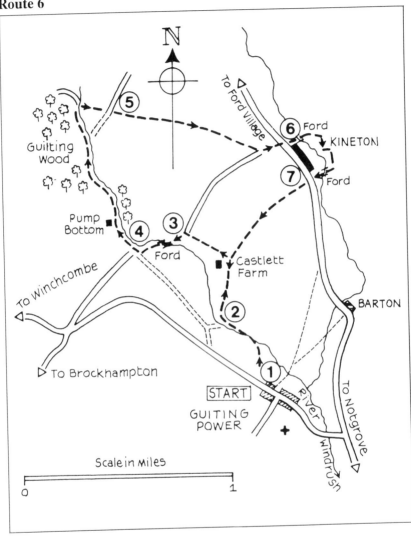

Route 6

Upper Windrush Valley   5 miles

Start

Village Hall car park along lane by green at Guiting Power. The village lies a mile north of the B4068 (Andoversford-Stow road), 2½ miles N.E. of its junction with the A436. (O.S. Sheet Landranger 163, G.R. 095248).

Route

1. *Walk back to the village street and turn left. After passing the post office, turn right along a lane. Keep on through a metal gate and follow a descending path through a second gate to the foot of the slope. Fork right here and after crossing a tiny footbridge, climb the slope and go through a handgate.*

2. *Follow the clearly-defined path towards Castlett Farm. Go through a handgate and bear left at a junction. Keep the farm on the left and follow the drive to meet a minor road. Turn left. (Beware traffic).*

3. *The lane soon dips to a ford, with a tiny footbridge alongside. Climb the slope and pass through a gate to meet a crossroads.*

4. *Turn right along a road signposted 'Unsuitable for motors'. Follow the road through a gate into a wood to the right of a cottage. The road follows the stream on the right as far as a T-junction. Turn right and climb to a crossways.*

5. *Leave the metalled road by keeping straight on along a rough track, which passes some farm buildings on the right and later a wood on the left to reach a road. Turn left and descend to a T-junction. Kineton lies to the right.*

6. *To cross the two fords on the infant Windrush, go down the first lane on the left and follow the narrow lane which climbs back to the main road just beyond the Half Way House Inn.*

7. *The footpath back to Castlett Farm starts on the right opposite the end of a long stone barn. Pass through a gateway with farm buildings on the right. The path keeps field boundaries on the left through three fields before crossing a stile into a garden to reach the outward route.*

Access by bus

Pulham's buses from Cheltenham (limited service).

Refreshments

Half Way House, Kineton. Morning coffee, Lunches. Children welcome. Garden.
Farmers Arms, Guiting Power. Morning coffee, Lunches. Children welcome. Garden.

Village Green, Lower Slaughter

Three Rivers Walk

Outline
Upper Slaughter - Lower Slaughter - Slaughter Bridge - Water Bridge - Salmonsbury - Bourton-on-the-Water - Lansdown - Bourton Bridge - Upper Slaughter.

Summary
The 3 rivers alluded to in the title of this walk - Eye, Dikler and Windrush - together with the villages on their banks, epitomise to many all that is best about the Cotswolds. The price paid by the villages for their popularity - crowds and congestion - is high, but this walk is routed to avoid most of the tripper traffic and to enable walkers to enjoy delightful countryside along footpaths and minor roads.

Attractions
So much praise has been heaped upon the Slaughters over the years that it serves little purpose to add to it here. The water mill on the River Eye at Lower Slaughter, with its oddly-alluring red-brick chimney, cannot fail to intrigue. There is often a beautiful sulphur-breasted grey wagtail on or near the water wheel, and the shallow water nearby provides safe, clean paddling for the young while the older browse along the village street.

Once the Fosse Way has been crossed, the crowds are left behind and the field paths to Bourton along the valley of the River Dikler, offer pleasant, easy walking. There are wild flowers in plenty in the damp meadows, including lady's smock (cuckoo flower) marsh marigold (king cup) and several species of orchid. There is also a chance to see the scanty remnant of the old Iron-age earthwork of Salmonsbury Camp near which iron currency bars, used as money by the inhabitants in pre-Roman times, were discovered during archaeological excavations. Birdwatching opportunities, too, arise where the route passes two of the ornamental lakes, complete with islands, which were created by the flooding of old gravel pits twenty or so years ago. Mute swans, Canada geese and coots are the likeliest birds to attract attention, the coots by their noisy calls as well as their contrasting black plumage and white head patches. The graceful necks of a pair of great-crested grebes may also capture the party's interest, especially in spring, when the birds face one another with raised ruffs during their courtship ritual. On no account should children be allowed into the water, as the sides of the pits are steeply-sloping and therefore extremely dangerous.

After refreshments at Bourton, there is another opportunity to paddle, this time in the largest of the three rivers. This is the Windrush, along the bank of which the walk continues to the Fosse Way at Bourton Bridge and beyond by the old railway embankment. Until about 1960, trains connected Bourton with Cheltenham and Banbury. There follows a delightful stretch of woodland walking before the route climbs steadily to conclude with a downhill mile along minor roads back to Upper Slaughter.

Other attractions
A few of Bourton's attractions are listed at the foot of Route 8.

Route 7

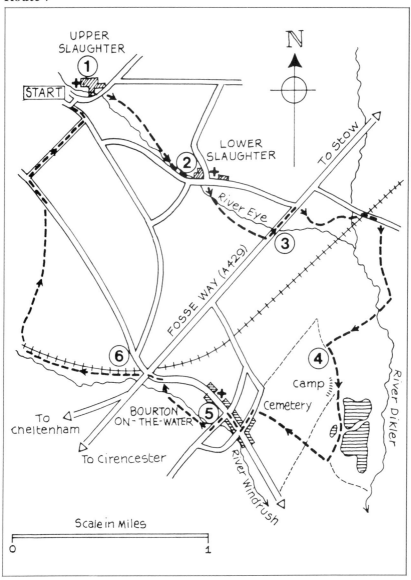

UPPER SLAUGHTER

START

N

LOWER SLAUGHTER

To Stow

River Eye

FOSSE WAY (A429)

To Cheltenham

BOURTON ON-THE-WATER

To Cirencester

Camp

Cemetery

River Dikler

River Windrush

Scale in Miles

0   1

Route 7

Three Rivers Walk   6 miles

Start

Car park at the centre of Upper Slaughter, a village 2 miles N.W. of Bourton-on-the-Water and midway between the A436 and the A429 (Fosse Way). O.S. Sheet Landranger 163, G.R. 155232.

Route

1. *From the car park, take the road signposted 'Ford. Unsuitable for motors'. Cross the River Eye by a footbridge and turn right along a road and right again over a bridge at a T-junction. In 100 metres, turn left along a signposted footpath. Cross a footbridge and go through a kissing gate before climbing half-right up a grassy bank topped by scattered trees. Go through a kissing gate under a fine oak tree and follow the well-worn riverside path to Lower Slaughter Mill.*

2. *Pass the mill and follow the river through the village. Beyond a road bridge, follow the riverside path and turn left over a stile along a signposted footpath, with the river now on the left. Cross 3 stiles to join the Fosse Way. Cross with great care and turn left along the pavement as far as a gate alongside a cottage, opposite the turn to the Slaughters.*

3. *Follow the track into a narrow field. Where it widens, follow the ill-defined raised track across the field over a bridge and through a gate. Turn right at a road, and after crossing a railway bridge turn right through the first of two gates sharing a wide entrance. Keep the hedge on the left as far as another gate, where the path switches to the other side of the hedge. Cross the River Dikler at a cart bridge and follow the Oxfordshire Way signs over 3 bridges to the top right-hand corner of a field. Pass through the kissing gate and turn left along a grassy lane, leaving the Oxfordshire Way.*

4. *Keep straight on along the lane passing the scanty remnants of Salmonsbury Camp on the right. Bear left, at a fork and follow waymarks to reach a lake. Keep the lake on the left and cross a stile to reach a path between two more lakes. When the path forks, turn right through a gate into a lane. Pass allotments and a cemetery before bearing left along a footpath just before a bus garage. Turn left again at the road into Bourton-on-the-Water.*

5. *Leave the village by crossing the Windrush by the war memorial. Soon, where the road forks, take the signposted footpath between houses on the right. Follow this path along the river bank and cross at Mill House, where the path meets a road. Turn left and follow the pavement to Bourton Bridge on the Fosse Way (A429).*

6. *Cross carefully and go through a handgate to follow a path with the river on the left. Keep straight on through gates with a wire fence on the left. Climb the old railway*

embankment and turn left along it for a short distance before veering right to follow the side of a wood to a gate. Turn right up a shady path, signposted 'Slaughters', and climb through fields to a road. Turn left (beware of traffic) and soon right along a minor road back to Upper Slaughter. Turn left at a T-junction and right along a footpath under a yew tree for a short cut back to the car park.

Refreshments

There are several cafes and inns at Bourton-on-the-Water.

Canada Goose
Brown, black and white. 100cm.

Bourton-on-the-Water Lakes

Outline
Rissington Bridge - Rissington Mill - Leasow Lane - Rissington Bridge.

Summary
Although they resemble lakes, the stretches of water around which this short walk is routed are in fact flooded pits formed during the 1960's and 1970's after the termination of gravel extraction along the Windrush and Dikler valleys. The pits are put to a variety of uses - one is now a carp farm, another is used for windsurfing and others are stocked with fish to provide sport for anglers. Fortunately, most of the pits are accessible along public footpaths and road walking is confined to a half-mile section midway along the route.

Attractions
The creation of this complex of lakes has greatly enriched the variety of wild life in the area around Bourton. ('On the Water' refers, of course, to its situation on the River Windrush). Natural history, therefore - plants, insects, and especially birds - provides the main attraction, and binoculars are strongly recommended. Muddy conditions are likely in wet weather, so wellingtons are also advisable.

The pits are steep-sided, deep and dangerous and on no account should children be allowed to approach the water's edge. In any case, most of the plants - reeds, sedges, iris, water mint, loosestrife, willow herb, and so on - can be identified from the footpath, and good views obtained of the host of dragonflies, damselflies, butterflies and grasshoppers.

But it is the bird life that can be relied upon to capture the interest of the majority of visitors, and this varies depending on the time of year. For sheer numbers, winter is the best time to visit, for during these months, the resident population of swans, coots, grebes, mallard and tufted duck is augmented by large flocks of visiting ducks, including wigeon and pochard, and by mixed parties of gulls. In recent years Canada geese have established themselves on some of the lakes and occasionally such unusual vagrants as a cormorant or a red-crested pochard can be seen.

During spring and summer, the skies above the lakes are alive with the darting shapes of swallows, martins and swifts, feeding on the myriads of tiny insects attracted by the large expanse of water. Two fish-eating birds, the grey heron and the brilliantly-coloured kingfisher, can be seen in the vicinity throughout the year, as can the pied and grey wagtail and the dipper, which favours the banks of the Dikler and Windrush. These rivers meet a short distance from the small lake on the last stage of the walk.

Other attractions
No visitor to Bourton, least of all a bird lover, should miss seeing Birdland, a unique collection of birds from many parts of the world, established by the late Len Hill. The village's other attractions - model village, butterfly collection, trout farm, car museum - are guaranteed to fill any time remaining.

Route 8

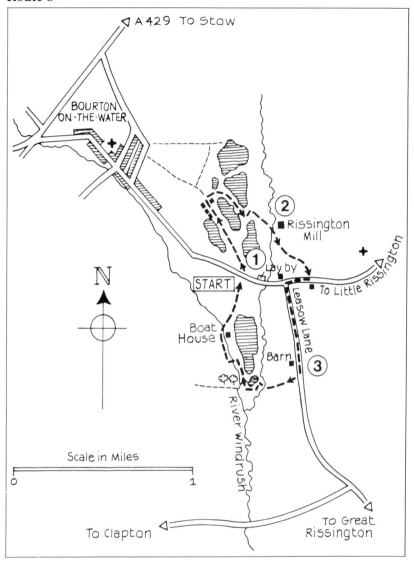

A 429 To Stow

BOURTON ON-THE-WATER

②

Rissington Mill

To Little Rissington

①

Lay by

START

N

Boat House

Barn

③

Leasow Lane

River Windrush

Scale in Miles

0   1

To Clapton

To Great Rissington

Route 8

Bourton-on-the-Water Lakes   3 miles

Start

Approaching from Bourton, at a lay-by along Rissington Road, just beyond the speed limit sign. Pull in on the left by a bend sign just before a bridge (O.S. Sheet Landranger 163, G.R. 180198).

Route

1. *Walk back along the pavement as far as the speed limit sign. Cross a stile in the hedge to another at the opposite corner of the field. Cross a plank bridge and a third stile and follow the path between two lakes. Beyond houses on the left, cross a stile straight ahead and turn right at a junction of tracks. Go through a gap by a gate and in 40 metres veer right at a fork along a narrow path between two lakes. This path, which can be muddy, bends to the left and crosses a footbridge to pass through a gate in the hedge on the right.*

2. *Cross a meadow to another stile and veer right along the river bank (The Dikler) to cross two footbridges by Rissington Mill. Follow the path round the mill grounds to reach a drive. Turn right along the drive, following it to reach a T-junction with the Rissington-Bourton road. Turn right along the pavement and cross with care to take the minor road signposted to Great Rissington.*

3. *In about half a mile, and about 100 metres beyond a barn on the right, turn right along a signposted footpath through a gate. Keep the hedge on the right over two fields and cross a gated bridge over the Dikler. Follow the path with the river on the left before veering to the right and through a handgate on the left to a small lake. Keeping the lake on the right, follow it round two sides to cross a stile by a gate. Continue to cross the Windrush by a footbridge and turn right over a stile. In 20 metres, cross another stile on the right and follow a path through scrub to reach a cart-bridge. Cross the Windrush once more and follow the track to a stile to the right of a cattle grid. Cross a field to a final stile and follow a track to the Rissington road. Turn right back to the lay-by.*

Access by bus

Pulham's Coaches connect Bourton-on-the-Water with Cheltenham, Stow-on-the-Wold and Moreton-in-Marsh.

Refreshments

There are numerous cafes and inns at Bourton-on-the-Water.

Brockhampton, The Old Brewery

Upper Coln Valley

Outline
Syreford - Sevenhampton - Brockhampton - Syreford.

Summary
The high ground on the flanks of Cleeve Common gives rise to a number of watercourses, the northern-flowing of which, including the rivers Isbourne and Swilgate, contribute their waters to the Severn. It is to the Thames however, that the loveliest and most renowned of these rivers, the Coln, makes its way. This walk traces the infant Coln upstream through the attractive villages of Sevenhampton and Brockhampton and returns along an ancient bridleway offering fine views over some of the best of unspoilt Cotswold landscape. The mile and a half of road walking is confined to minor roads.

Attractions
Fields, woods, stone walls, hedges - all clinging to the slopes of a tiny valley, along which flows a pure, tinkling stream. The stream is, of course, the river Coln, hastening on its urgent, youthful way, to the glories of Chedworth Roman villa and idyllic Bibury many a twisting mile downstream.

Leaving tiny Syreford, where many secrets of an extensive Roman settlement remain yet to be uncovered, the walk enters the long strip of Syreford Plantation, a mixed woodland in which the carpet of dog's mercury, enchanter's nightshade and twayblade suggests that there was an ancient wood here long before the present gnarled and towering trees began to take root.

Sevenhampton, reached by a field path from which glimpses of the tiny river can be had in the valley below, has a delightful ford, guaranteed to prove an irresistible diversion. The village is in two parts, that containing the lovely little Norman church of St. Andrew being tucked away on the opposite bank, where it can be reached by a short detour. The route keeps straight on along the right bank, following a narrow metalled lane, which climbs steadily up to Brockhampton.

Although bigger and easier of access than its neighbour, Brockhampton was for centuries merely a hamlet within Sevenhampton parish. The inn and the old brewery lie down a back lane to the left of the junction of the lane with the main village street, while beyond lies Brockhampton Court, a 17th-century mansion later enlarged and now converted into residential apartments.

The climb up the slope to reach the bridleway can be made easier and more pleasant by following the minor roads by Baker's Wood, which entails adding a mere half-mile or so to the route. The descent along the bridleway back to Syreford provides the opportunity not only to enjoy the sweeping views but also to watch out for a range of lime-loving wild flowers and the butterflies which they attract. Among the birds, skylarks rise to sing overhead and pheasants, partridges, woodpigeons and a variety of smaller species provide plenty of interest as the old track winds its way down the slope back to Syreford.

Route 9

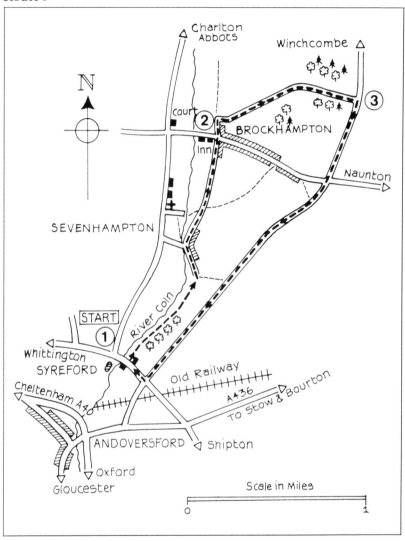

Charlton Abbots

Winchcombe

N

court

②

BROCKHAMPTON

③

Inn

Naunton

SEVENHAMPTON

River Coln

START
①

Whittington
SYREFORD

Old Railway

Cheltenham A40

A436

To Stow & Bourton

ANDOVERSFORD

Shipton

Oxford

Gloucester

Scale in Miles

0   1

42

Route 9

Upper Coln Valley   5½ miles

Start

The hamlet of Syreford, just off the A436, a mile north-east of Andoversford. (O.S. Sheet Landranger 163, G.R. 029204). Cars should be parked on the grass verge near the old railway embankment.

Route

1. *Follow the footpath through a gateway between a barn and stables, opposite a house near which a stream flows by an old millstone. The footpath is in fact a grassy track as far as some houses, after which it enters a wood. After leaving the wood, cross two fields to pass through a metal gate on the left into a grassy lane, between stone walls. Pass through a second gate into Sevenhampton. (A short diversion is possible here by the ford to visit the church - see map). Otherwise, follow the lane straight on, signposted 'Unsuitable for motor vehicles', up to Brockhampton.*

2. *The Craven Arms Inn lies to the left of the lane's junction with the village street. To continue the walk, cross the street at the junction and follow the lane opposite which, after passing several houses, bends to the right and continues for about a mile through wooded countryside to a T-junction.*

3. *Turn right along another minor road, which in half a mile climbs to another T-junction. Cross here to follow the bridleway, which descends for about two miles through fields to meet the road at Syreford near the old railway embankment. The starting point lies to the right.*

Access by bus

Pulham's bus service (Bourton-on-the-Water to Cheltenham). Some buses are routed through Brockhampton.

Refreshments

The Craven Arms Inn, Brockhampton.

Bar meals and restaurant. Garden. Children welcome.

Enchanter's Nightshade
White. June-Sept.

43

The Green, Cold Aston

Wold Villages Walk

Outline

Hazleton - Notgrove - Cold Aston - Turkdean - Hazleton.

Summary

This walk, the longest of the selection, will provide a challenge to families wishing to pit their energies against a somewhat more demanding route. The going is, by Cotswold standards, a little rough in places, especially after rain, but this is more than compensated for by the wide, lonely atmosphere of the wolds, which can best be savoured along little-used trackways well away from the roads. The walk takes in four typical Cotswold upland villages, each with its own distinctive features, which, if time permits, can be enjoyed on the way. These villages can, of course, be visited by car; seen as part of a long wold walk however, they take on an entirely different perspective.

Attractions

The four villages visited on this walk all lie off main roads and retain much of their old-world appeal, without being in any way tourist showpieces. They each possess a church containing considerable Norman traces, and houses and barns also many centuries old. The barns in particular, are well worth studying in some detail. Like the farmhouses and other buildings, they are constructed of locally-quarried limestone, although some have lost their original stone-slated roofs. These have been replaced either by imported grey slates, an assortment of tiles, or even in some cases, by corrugated iron, though happily these are comparatively few. The barn doorways were built sufficiently large to allow the great ox-drawn harvest wagons to enter, while the smaller doors opposite were used by the leaving empty wagons. It is sometimes possible to peep inside and see the great roughly-fashioned beams supporting the roof. Many barns had dovecotes built into their gables, a reminder that these birds provided a useful source of meat in bygone times. Most of these old barns are still in use in some way or other and are kept in good repair.

Sheep farming plays a vital role in the Cotswolds, as it has done for centuries. Nowadays, meat production, rather than wool, dominates, however, and the traditional Cotswold sheep have been succeeded by other breeds. Herds of cattle can also be seen on the walk, although the main form of land-use is crop production, chiefly barley and wheat, and this has resulted in the forming of larger fields for more efficient harvesting, and also in the ploughing up of some of the old footpaths.

Pheasants are a common sight on this walk. They are reared for shooting and are fed on grain from old milk churns and oil drums. This is why they appear more like tame birds than wild ones. Whatever we may think of pheasant-shooting as a sport, it remains, like fox hunting, a thriving pastime in the Cotswolds.

Nearby attraction

Cotswold Countryside Collection, Northleach. This museum, based at the former prison, provides a valuable insight into the evolution of rural life in the Cotswolds over the centuries. It is open throughout the summer months.

Route 10

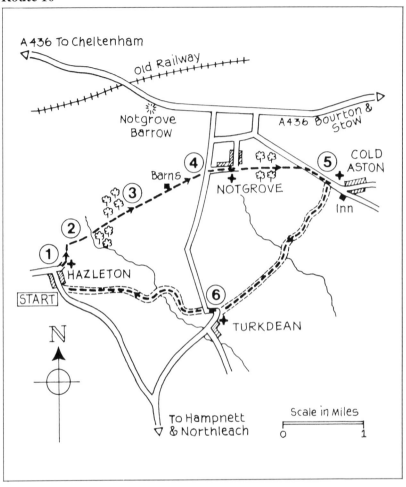

A 436 To Cheltenham

old Railway

Notgrove
Barrow

A436 Bourton &
Stow

COLD
ASTON

④ Barns

⑤

NOTGROVE

Inn

③

②

①

HAZLETON

START

⑥

TURKDEAN

N

To Hampnett
& Northleach

Scale in miles

0   1

46

Route 10

Wold Villages Walk   8 miles

Start

Hazleton village, one mile north of the A40 and 3½ miles N.W. of Northleach. (O.S. Sheet Landranger 163, G.R. 080182). Parking is available on the grass verge on the edge of the village.

Route

1. *Follow the lane with the 'No through road' sign by the church. There are modern bungalows on the left but fine views away to the right. Go on through 2 gates towards farm buildings.*

2. *Immediately after crossing a cattle grid, turn right along a grassy track with a wood on the right and a grassy bank on the left. Near the end of the wood go through a gateway and climb up the bank on the left through the scrub, keeping a barbed wire fence on the left. Go through a metal gate in a wire fence and turn right along the edge of the field, following it round to pass through another metal gate at the top of the field. Cross the next field, aiming for the left-hand corner of the wood ahead. (Barns can be seen to the right beyond).*

3. *Follow the wood side along the edge of the field, aiming for the barns. Pass through a handgate at the corner of the field by the side of the wood and descend along the edge of the next field under the trees to another gate in the hollow. Climb up the slope past the barns to a road.*

4. *Turn left and then right into Notgrove. Keep straight on along a lane towards the church. Beyond, where the lane bends to the left in a hollow, turn right through a gate into a field. Climb to the top of the field, making for a gate in a stone wall with an avenue of trees in the background. Turn right along the track to another gate on the left leading through the avenue. Follow the path to a road.*

5. *Turn right towards Aston Blank (Cold Aston). The route continues along a metalled track on the right, just beyond the village sign, and signposted 'Unsuitable for Motors'. (Note: to see the village and/or to visit the Plough Inn, keep straight ahead). The metalled track reverts eventually to a roughly-surfaced track for 2 miles to Turkdean.*

6. *At Turkdean, the track meets a road. To return to Hazleton, turn right and then left in 30 metres along a track past farm buildings. In the valley bottom, instead of keeping straight on through a gate, turn left over a stream and through another gate to follow the track up past a farm to Hazleton.*

Shorter variations

The walk can be shortened by omitting one or more of the villages on the route by following roads shown on the map.

Refreshments

The Plough Inn, Cold Aston. Morning coffee, lunches. Children welcome.

Coberley Church and Hall Ruins

Churn Valley

Outline

Seven Springs - Upper Coberley - Cockleford - Cowley - Coberley -Seven Springs.

Summary

Although quite near to Cheltenham, this walk follows quiet footpaths and country roads throughout its entire course. The Churn, which rises at Seven Springs, is the river upon which Cirencester stands, and some local people still claim it as the true Thames. The early part of the walk provides fine views of the valley, while the later stages offer the chance to get to know the upper reaches of this lovely river, with its lakes and ornamental waters, as well as something of the history of this little-known corner of the Cotswolds.

Attractions

Seven Springs, the source of the Churn, is reached by stone steps descending from the lay-by. In the hollow beneath the beech trees, an inscription on the stonework, translated from the Latin, reads:

'Here, O father Thames, thy sevenfold spring'

That there are in fact seven springs will have to be taken on trust, but children may be quite surprised by the comparison of this tiny trickle with the size of the river at Tomtit's Bottom, a mere three miles downstream.

The bridleway to and from Upper Coberley provides the only hill-walking on the route. Cowley and Coberley can be picked out from the crest, and some idea obtained of the effects of enclosures on the landscape, by the patchwork of fields on the opposite side of the valley. The bridge by the millhouse at Tomtit's Bottom is an ideal spot for the young bird-watcher. Dippers sometimes fly low along the river and there is a chance that a grey wagtail may appear.

Cowley Manor was once the home of the Horlick family, makers of a popular bedtime drink, and their family initials can still be seen on some of the buildings in the village. Lewis Carroll, creator of Alice in Wonderland, often stayed at the rectory with his uncle, accompanied by young Alice Liddell, on whom Alice was based. Today, Cowley is known for its campsite, used by Girl Guides and Brownies from all over Gloucestershire.

The wild life of the Cowley region has been captured on tape by a local farmer, Ray Goodwin, whose recordings of the private lives of animals, ranging in size from badgers down to wasps and beetles, have won him the title of Wildlife Sound Recordist for the whole of Britain.

continued on page 52

Route 11

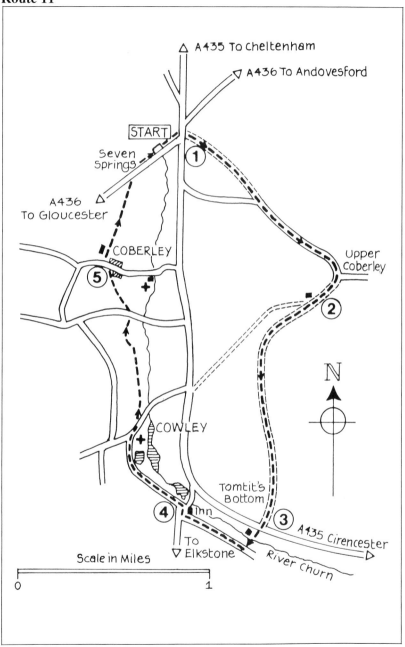

△ A435 To Cheltenham

▽ A436 To Andovesford

START

Seven Springs

①

A436
To Gloucester △

COBERLEY

Upper Coberley

⑤ ✠

②

COWLEY ✠

N

Tomtit's Bottom

④ Inn

③ A435 Cirencester ▷

To ▽ Elkstone

River Churn

Scale in Miles

0   1

Route 11

Churn Valley   6½ miles

Start

Lay-by at Seven Springs, a short distance along the A436 west of the junction with the A435, 4 miles south of Cheltenham. (O.S. Sheet Landranger 163, G.R. 170968).

Route

1. *Walk to the junction of the two main roads. Cross with great care and take the rough gated track climbing to the right by the crossroads. Bear left along a road. Ignore the bridleway and footpath to Wistley Hill on the left. Continue to a fork by a cottage and turn right into Upper Coberley.*

2. *Beyond the gateway at Lower Farm, turn left up a rough track. At its crest, Cowley (left) and Coberley (right) can be seen in the valley below. Descend past a farm to the A435.*

3. *Cross the busy road with great care and pass through the gateway opposite (by a postbox). Descend the mill-house drive to cross the River Churn by a delightful little bridge. This is called Tomtit's Bottom (boundless scope for speculation!). Climb the track to a minor road. Turn right, and at a T-junction, right again, to the Green Dragon Inn.*

4. *Take the minor road opposite the inn. Turn right into Cowley at a junction (Edward VII postbox in wall opposite). At a right-hand bend, after passing the church and manor, keep straight on along a track signposted 'Churnside Camp'. Cross a stile into a field to a second stile and make for a gap in the hedge ahead. Through the gap, keep the hedge on the left and after the path has veered to the right, go through a gap to the left, marked by a yellow arrow, and descend to cross a footbridge over a stream. The path now skirts the left-hand edge of an orchard and dips down to cross a track between two stiles. In the next field, head half-left towards Coberley, clearly visible ahead, reaching the village by crossing a stile and stone-slabbed bridge.*

5. *The diversion to the church should be made here. (Signboard on wall). To continue the walk, cross the road through the safety barrier and after passing the cross and the school on the left, follow the grassy track ahead, signposted 'Seven Springs'. Ignore a path to the left, keeping straight on with a hedge on the right. Bear right over a stile to meet the A436. The lay-by is on the right.*

Refreshments

Green Dragon Inn, Cockleford. Lunches served. Children welcome.

Coberley, though small, also has plenty of interest. It is well worth making a short diversion to see the church of St. Giles. This is approached through a gatehouse of the long-since demolished Coberley Hall, in which once lived the youthful Dick Whittington, later to become Lord Mayor of London. Dick's mother, Lady Joan Berkeley, is buried in the church, and her stone effigy can be seen. Another interesting monument is that to Sir Giles de Berkeley, who died in 1295, and whose heart was buried here, although his body was interred at Little Malvern. This is the only heart burial known in the Cotswolds.

Outside, in the churchyard, youngsters, especially of the pony-mad variety, may enjoy looking for the stone to Lombard, Sir Giles' horse, near the remains of the wall of the old hall.

Old Railway Bridge, Chedworth Village (now demolished)

Chedworth Woods and Roman Villa

Outline

Chedworth Roman Villa - Chedworth Woods - Chedworth Village - Chedworth Roman Villa.

Summary

This short walk is intended to allow for a combined visit to Chedworth Roman Villa (National Trust) and the surrounding woods. It also takes in the village of Chedworth, where a pub lunch is available. For those wishing to extend the visit, a short walk along the River Coln, involving a retracing of steps, or road walking, is also included.

Although only short, the woodland walk can be muddy after rain, so stout footwear is strongly recommended. It is of course, possible to devote the entire visit to a woodland ramble, omitting the villa, for although the woods are private, there are plenty of footpaths to follow.

At the time of writing, the villa is open every day except Monday between March and October from 10am to 5.30pm. Check winter open times by ringing 01242 890256

Attractions

The villa stands in a superb woodland setting on a hillside overlooking the River Coln. It is said to have been discovered last century by a gamekeeper digging to retrieve a lost ferret and is generally considered to be one of the best-preserved relics of its kind in the country. It has over 30 rooms, arranged around two courtyards, and facing down the valley. Children who consider washing an irksome chore may be impressed to see the Romans' sophisticated bathing arrangements - two bath-houses, one providing damp heat in the style of a Turkish bath, the other somewhat like a modern sauna. Under-floor heating was by means of a well-preserved hypocaust. In addition, covered mosaics can be inspected and there is an excellent little museum.

The woods, part of an extensive tract stretching as far as Yanworth and Withington, comprise some of the oldest and most valuable woodland habitat in the Cotswolds. The wild life, especially the flora, is extremely rich and varied and families particularly interested in identifying wild flowers should come equipped with a suitable book. Trees, shrubs, flowering plants, ferns, fungi, lichens - all these abound along the woodland paths, and young botanists are assured of a rewarding walk whatever the time of year.

Another interesting feature of the woods is the old railway line. This long-disused track once extended along much of the Coln valley, linking Cirencester with Andoversford junction, from where trains connected with Cheltenham and Banbury. The dismantled line, overgrown and almost forgotten, is now a nature reserve, administered by the Gloucestershire Wildlife Trust, with wild life flourishing where trains once puffed their noisy and smokey way. The geological sections are also of considerable interest.

continued on page 56

53

Route 12

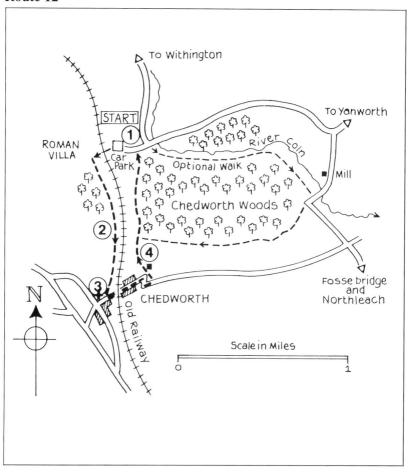

To Withington

To Yanworth

START

1

ROMAN
VILLA

Car
Park

River Coln

Mill

Optional Walk

Chedworth Woods

2

4

N

3

Old Railway

CHEDWORTH

Fosse bridge
and
Northleach

Scale in Miles

0   1

Route 12

Chedworth Woods and Roman Villa

3 miles
(Plus optional river walk)

Start

At Chedworth Villa car park.

*Note: the villa is **not** at Chedworth village. It lies approximately between Chedworth and Yanworth, 5 miles W.S.W. of Northleach, and is best approached from the A429 (Fosse Way) between Fossebridge and Northleach crossroads. Watch for signs. (O.S. Sheet Landranger 163, G.R. 053135).*

Route

1. *From the villa entrance, follow the 'Public Footpath' sign into the woods, crossing under the line of the old railway and climb to the first cross track. Turn left. Ignore minor paths to left and right, keeping straight on until the path leaves the woods over a stile.*

2. *Follow the path ahead to reach 2 handgates beneath a sycamore tree. Go through the right-hand gate and, ignoring a wooden stile on the left, cross a stone one straight ahead and descend the steps under the trees. Enter a long field. Chedworth lies straight ahead. Make for the village, to cross a stile by the first cottage on the right. The church is straight ahead and the Seven Tuns Inn beyond on the slope to the left*

3. *Facing the inn, turn left down the hill through the village (beware traffic). Climb the hill out of Chedworth, passing the drive to Hartshill Farm. At the top of the hill, follow the bridleway sign on the left indicating the Roman villa.*

4. *On reaching a barn, pass through the left hand of 2 gates to go through another gate. This point is the meeting of several paths. To continue the route, take the field path directly opposite the stile on the left above a farm (i.e. the middle of 3 paths). This path descends to enter Chedworth woods. Follow the green marker posts through a handgate to reach the villa approach road and car park.*

Extending the Route

Go down to the junction of the villa approach road with the Withington-Yanworth road and turn right through a gateway along a private road (public footpath). This follows the River Coln, skirting the woodland fringe for about 1½ miles. Those with boundless energy may wish to walk the full distance and either retrace their steps or return by minor roads (an extra mile entailed by turning left at the end of the private road and left again in ¾ mile).

Chedworth is a pleasant, if somewhat straggling village, and well worth exploring. The church, like so many in the Cotswolds, dates from Norman times, and has several interesting features. Beware of traffic along the narrow, winding roads. Young members of parties embarking on the optional river walk may well like to investigate the workings of the hinges and catch of the gate at the entrance to the riverside footpath. (Please leave the gate as you found it afterwards!).

Refreshments
Seven Tuns, Chedworth. Lunches and coffee. Children welcomed.

Painswick Churchyard

56

Around Painswick

Outline

Painswick - Damsells Mill - Tocknell's Court - Royal William Inn - Painswick Beacon - Painswick.

Summary

Architecturally, Painswick is one of the gems among Cotswold towns and the surrounding countryside offers some of the finest walking in the entire region. The route is planned to enjoy the best of both, starting and finishing near the town's famous churchyard and including the valley of the Painswick Stream and the bracing upland stretch of Cotswold Way walking over Painswick Beacon. The walk ends with a gentle descent through golf greens with wide views towards the wooded slopes of Sheepscombe and Slad, immortalised by Laurie Lee in 'Cider with Rosie'.

Attractions

'Painswick Proud' is well named, for this little town of silvery-grey stone has survived the decline of its cloth industry, fighting between Cavaliers and Roundheads in the Civil War, and German bombs in the Second World War. Just over a century ago, a third of the fine steeple of St. Mary's church was destroyed by lightning, but today, fully restored, it rises 174 feet above what must be one of the most fascinating churchyards in England. The challenge here is to count the celebrated yew trees, planted nearly 200 years ago, and said to number 99. Local legend has it that attempts to plant a hundredth tree ended in failure. Why? No one seems to know. Every September, the children of Painswick join hands to encircle their church, an ancient ceremony known as Clipping. Although the churchyard yews are clipped at around this time, the tradition dates back much further, taking its name from a Saxon word, *clyppan*, meaning to embrace.

Painswick has many fine old buildings lining its narrow streets. Among the more interesting, and spanning several centuries, are The Chur, Pound House, Hazelbury House and the Little Fleece. Other notable buildings passed along the course of the walk include Damsells Mill, which at different times wove cloth and ground corn, and Tocknell's Court, over 300 years old, and possessing beautiful gardens.

Apart from the hazard of golf balls, the last stretch of the route over Painswick Hill provides ideal family walking. Wild flowers and butterflies abound and the hummocky ground in the vicinity of the Kimsbury Iron Age Fort, where King Charles' army spent an unhappy night after the siege of Gloucester, is perfectly suited to games of hide and seek and similar energy-consuming pastimes.

Route 13

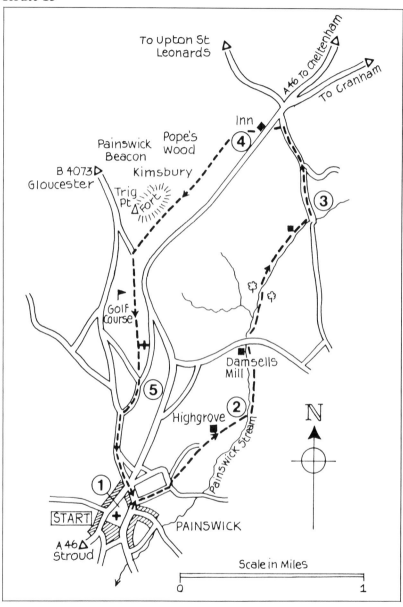

To Upton St
Leonards

A 46 To Cheltenham

To Cranham

Inn
④

Pope's
Wood

Painswick
Beacon

③

Kimsbury

B 4073
Gloucester

Trig
Pt   Fort

Golf
Course

Damsells
Mill

⑤

②

Highgrove

Painswick Stream

N

①

START

PAINSWICK

A 46
Stroud

Scale in Miles

0   1

58

Route 13

Around Painswick   5 miles

Start
The Stamages Lane car park at Painswick, just off the A46. Painswick is 3 miles north of Stroud. (O.S. Sheet Landranger 162, G.R. 866096).

Route

1. *Walk through the churchyard and after seeing the stocks outside the churchyard wall, walk along St. Mary's Street and turn right down Vicarage Street. After passing a lane on the right, follow a farm track also on the right alongside Museum Cottage. 100 metres down the lane, cross a stile on the right and follow the field path over another stile to reach the lane once more. Turn right and cross a stile to the right of Highgrove House. Keep straight on through a gateway into a field.*

2. *Keep the hedge on the right and pass through another gate. Cross a bridge and turn left to follow a marked footpath on the right bank of the stream to Damsells Mill. Cross a road and go over a stile opposite. Keep the stream on the left through 3 fields to enter a wood. Cross the stream near where the water cascades through an archway and bear right to pass a cottage. In 30 metres, go through a gate on the left and cross a field to Tocknell's Court. Cross a stile and keep to the right hand bank of the stream to reach a road.*

3. *Turn left for a steep climb up to the Royal William Inn, taking a short cut through the trees to the left when the signpost on the main road comes into view.*

4. *To return to Painswick, climb the lane by the inn. Fork right at a junction of paths and follow the Cotswold Way signs (white circles and coloured arrows) over golf greens, skirting a coniferous wood on the left as far as a road. Turn left, and in a short distance take the path signposted Painswick, passing Catsbrain quarry. The path descends through a wood and crosses another golf green before following a course parallel to the cemetery wall. Beyond the wall, cross another green, then a road to reach another road through some trees.*

5. *Turn right to meet the main road, then left as far as Gloucester Road. From the junction of this road with New Street, turn right for the car park.*

Refreshments
The Royal William Inn, Cranham. Morning coffee, Lunches. Children welcomed. Games room.
There are numerous cafes and inns in Painswick.

The Stocks, Painswick

Ford at Duntisbourne Leer

Route 14   5½ miles (Detour to Highwayman Inn - 2 miles extra)
Duntisbourne and Winstone

Outline
Duntisbourne Leer - Duntisbourne Abbots - Winstone - Gaskill's Farm - Duntisbourne Leer.

Summary
This walk, which follows tracks and footpaths for all but a mile or so of its course, through the valley of the Duntisbourne brook, offers easy, if not exactly spectacular walking. It takes in two of the four villages named after the modest stream, as well as the higher and somewhat bleak village of Winstone, and serves as a pleasant introduction to this often overlooked corner of the Cotswolds.

Attractions
Most children - of all ages - love water, and the tiny hamlet of Duntisbourne Leer offers it in plenty. There are two fords, crossing places along the Duntisbourne brook, or River Dunt as it is sometimes rather flatteringly called. The first, at the foot of the slope from the Roman Ermine Street, now the bustling A417, is a delightful spot, a place where all the family will want to linger, watching the ducks from the nearby farmyard dabbling, disturbed only by the occasional car. The second ford, tucked away along the lane leading to Duntisbourne Abbots, is an elongated affair, more like a trough rather than a mere water splash, and created by diverting the brook to run along the road, for the purpose of washing horses' hooves and cart wheels. Pedestrians can pass dry-shod along the adjacent causeway, but for adventurous children this ford presents irresistible possibilities!

Duntisbourne Abbots, largest by far of the four villages bearing the name of the stream, is an attractive place. Although rather heavily restored, the church of St. Peter contains a good deal of Norman work and many of the cottages are very old. The spotting of datestones and blocked doorways may prove an interesting diversion here. There is a youth hostel in the village and parties of young people can often be seen engaged in field studies in the neighbourhood.

The little church of St. Bartholomew at Winstone is even older than its neighbour, dating back to Saxon times. The churchyard contains a 14th-century cross and there are some interesting gravestones. Several of the village farms have old barns, some with dovecotes.

Those families seeking refreshment will need to make a detour of a mile or so each way from Winstone to the Highwayman Inn, situated alongside the A417. The chance to see the brightly-painted stage coach preserved in the inn grounds may serve as an incentive for tired youngsters.

The bridleway from beyond Gaskill's Farm provides pleasant, easy walking for the return journey, with birds and wild flowers to enjoy and glimpses of the gentle lowland Cotswold scene visible beyond the hedges. Although for variety the suggested route takes the upper lane back to Duntisbourne Leer from the end of the bridleway, a further chance to sample the diverted brook ford can be taken instead.

Route 14

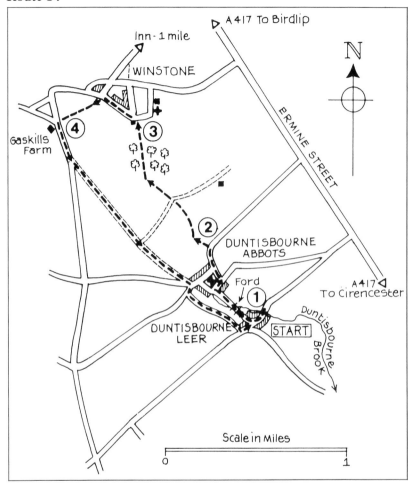

Route 14

Duntisbourne and Winstone   5½ miles
(Detour to Highwayman Inn - 2 miles extra)

Start

Duntisbourne Leer, a village a mile west of the A417 (Ermin Way), midway between Cirencester and Birdlip. Cars should be parked outside the village, preferably on the grass verge. (O.S. Sheet Landranger 163, G.R. 975075).

Route

1. *After seeing the ford at the foot of the village, climb the street and turn right along a lane signposted 'Unsuitable for Motor Vehicles'. Follow the causeway alongside the second ford and continue along the road to a crossroads at Duntisbourne Abbots. Cross, and after passing the church on the left, turn right at a junction. At the foot of the slope, turn left along a footpath signposted to Winstone.*

2. *Follow the path along a dry valley to a stile in the hedge. Pass through a handgate and cross a concrete road to go through another handgate directly opposite. On passing through a third handgate, a wood is seen ahead. Pass through a gate to the left of the wood. Eventually there is woodland on either side and beyond, the route crosses a field to a stile to the right of a farm.*

3. *This is Winstone. The church is on the right, but the route bears left, passing a fine buttressed barn. (Those wishing to visit the Highwayman Inn should turn right here to follow a signposted footpath and so cut down road walking). Keep straight on through the village as far as a footpath sign to the left near a road junction, almost opposite the old school. Follow this footpath across a field to a gate opposite, passing a pond and trough on the right. From the gate, cross a field, aiming for the centre of a group of farm buildings, to reach a road over a stile.*

4. *Turn left along the road. Soon, a track on the left is reached, signposted 'Duntisbourne Abbots. Unsuitable for Motors'. Follow this track back to the village. Return to the car by turning right at the end of the track for a short distance along the road, and then left for the last half-mile back to Duntisbourne Leer. Alternatively, those wishing to return by way of the diverted brook ford passed on the outward route can do so by descending to the left and then turning right.*

Refreshments

The Highwayman, Beechpike, Elkstone. Lunches served. Children welcomed. Games room.

Arlington Row, Bibury

Lower Coln Valley

Outline
Bibury - Coln St. Aldwyns - Arlington Row - Bibury.

Summary
Bibury, once described by the writer and craftsman William Morris as the most beautiful village ·in England, remains an enchanting place despite all the traffic and trappings associated with tourism. Much of its charm derives from the River Coln, more beguiling even than it was upstream at Chedworth. This route follows the Coln on its Thames-bound journey as far as Coln St. Aldwyns, another most attractive village, and returns along footpaths and bridleways over gently undulating park and farmland, as pleasant walking as any to be found in the south-east Cotswolds.

Attractions
Both young and old are fascinated by rivers and the 'Clear Coln', as an early poet described it, cannot fail to delight the young bird-watcher, botanist and insect-spotter. Dippers dart along above the rippling water, herons fish in the shallows, and moorhens and mallard can be heard and spotted by keen eyes among the waterside plants. The bird life of Bibury itself is chiefly of the domesticated variety, only too willing to be fed by younger children, but once the centre of the village has been left behind, their wild relatives take over.

The Coln is, of course, a trout stream, and its fishing rights are jealously guarded. There is no harm in looking however, and sharp eyes will pick out the trout, especially during spring and early summer when they leap out of the water in their determination to catch the juicy hovering mayflies. No man loved the Coln more than J. Arthur Gibbs, the young Victorian squire of nearby Ablington. In 1898, just before his tragically early death, he published his only book, 'A Cotswold Village', which is full of observations on country life in the area. Returning from Coln St. Aldwyns, the route passes between Coneygar Farm and Coneygar Wood. Coney is an old word for a rabbit and according to Gibbs, this indicated a place where rabbits could be found. It is worth noticing whether this is still true.

In bygone times, most Cotswold rivers had their water mills and the Coln was no exception. A fine example can be seen at Coln St. Aldwyns and another at Bibury. The latter has been restored and opened to the public as a museum and art gallery. There is plenty here to interest every member of the family.

The long row of quaint little cottages called Arlington Row, passed on the final stage of the walk, were once the homes of cloth weavers. They were placed under the care of the National Trust after a rich American tried to buy them to ship them across the Atlantic! Nearby, a marshy meadow called Rack Isle was so named because it was formerly used for the racks of cloth put out to dry after being fulled, or cleansed at the mill.

Attractions at Bibury
Arlington Mill Museum. The Trout Farm. Saxon church. Village lockup. Old dovecote.

Route 15

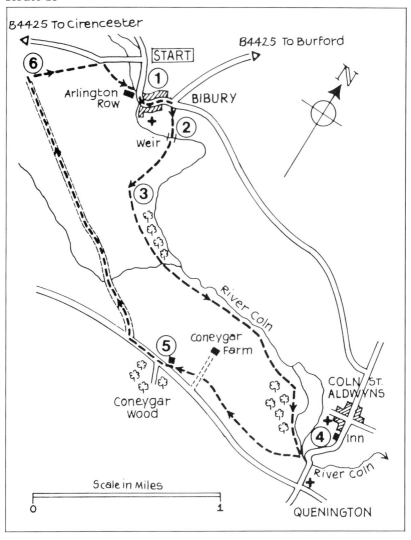

B4425 To Cirencester

B4425 To Burford

START

⑥

①

Arlington Row

BIBURY

②

weir

③

④

⑤

Coneygar Farm

Coneygar Wood

COLN ST. ALDWYNS

Inn

River Coln

River Coln

QUENINGTON

Scale in Miles

0   1

N

66

Route 15

Lower Coln Valley   6½ miles

Start

The village of Bibury, on the B4425, 7 miles N.E. of Cirencester. (O.S. Sheet Landranger 163, G.R. 115067). Parking is available in the village.

Route

1. *Follow the riverside pavement of the B4425 (signposted Aldsworth and Burford), ignoring 3 tempting right turns. At the fourth turn, signposted Coln St. Aldwyns, turn right, and in a short distance, take a signposted bridleway on the right to pass Bibury Court Farm.*

2. *Cross a bridge with a weir on the right and follow the road through the farm buildings. Keep straight on, ignoring a footpath on the right, through 2 gates and at a fork, bear left. Where the main track bends to the right, keep straight on along a grassy track with a wood on the left. After passing through a gate, the route continues as a footpath along the left-hand edge of a field to a handgate, from which it dips to a stile and a ditch. Cross and bear half-left, aiming for the left-hand edge of a wood opposite. The path passes through 2 gates between the wood and the river. At the end of the wood, follow the line of the river, first across grassland and then arable.*

3. *When another wood appears ahead, veer towards it, along the edge of a narrow field, as estate signs indicate. After skirting part of the wood the path enters the trees, to emerge once more by the river at Coln St. Aldwyns, which is entered through a gate by a cottage at the end of the field.*

4. *(Return route). From the cottage, follow the bridleway sign up a grassy bank under the trees and go through a metal gate. The route soon follows a wall on the left and passes through a metal gate. Cross a field, aiming between a house and some barns. Pass through a gateway in a wall and straight on to reach a track through a gate near a house. Cross this track to a gate ahead, to the right of a double power post. Cross a field, aiming for a house ahead with trees on either side.*

5. *Reach a road through a gate to the left of the house and turn right for a short distance before taking a signposted footpath on the right (which is in fact a track). Follow this track for about 1½ miles as far as a crossroads of tracks, at which point, houses can be seen in the distance ahead to the right.*

6. *Turn right and follow the edge of a field as far as a 5-fingered signpost. Keep straight ahead through a gate and along a drive to a road junction. Turn right to pass Arlington Row and return to the starting point.*

Refreshments

The New Inn, Coln St. Aldwyns; Catherine Wheel, Arlington, Bibury.

Daneway Inn, Sapperton

Thames – Severn Canal

Outline

Chalford - Daneway - Oakridge - Oakridge Lynch - Chalford.

Summary

Canal-towpath walking is both easy and full of interest, even when, as in this case, the canal has been derelict for many years. The route begins with a 3-mile length of the 29-miles-long waterway linking the Thames and Severn, our two largest rivers, which was completed in 1789. After a break for refreshment at the Daneway Inn, canal addicts may wish to follow the towpath a further ¾ mile to see the mouth of the Sapperton tunnel, at 3,817 yards, the longest in Britain at the time of its construction. The return route, through woodland and along switchback paths and lanes, before dropping back to the Frome valley, provides a pleasant contrast for those reluctant to retrace their steps.

Attractions

Chalford is a steeply-terraced village on the north bank of the river Frome, this stretch of which is known as the Golden Valley. Donkeys carrying panniers once travelled its streets, many of which are even now unsuitable for cars. Rich cloth merchants' houses are scattered over the upper slopes, while weavers' cottages cluster lower down. The mills which once flourished along the valley have been converted to other uses since the cloth industry declined.

The remains of several old locks can be seen from the canal towpath. Altogether, 44 of these were needed to carry boats over the Cotswolds when the canal was working. Water-loss was always a problem, however, and the canal was finally abandoned in 1927. The Daneway Inn was once known as the Bricklayer's Arms, having served as living quarters for the 'navvies' - the name given to the men working on the navigation, as the canal was then called. These men had the difficult task of lining the tunnel walls and roof to ensure that they were safe. The towpath did not extend through the tunnel, which meant that the boatmen had to 'leg' their vessels through, lying on their backs and pushing with their feet on the tunnel roof.

It is hard to realise, standing on the towpath overlooking this overgrown waterway, that it was once a scene of bustling activity, with laden narrowboats, as the vessels were called, plying to and fro with cargoes of coal and raw materials for the local woollen mills. As well as the inn, there were wharves, warehouses and stables, together with the cottages to house the lengthmen, whose job it was to maintain the canal. A writer of 80 years ago describes the scene: 'For more than 3 miles the canal divides the wooded hills, a band of silver drawn through this valley of gold. Lock by Lock it mounts the gentle incline until it reaches the pound to Sapperton tunnel and at the summit passes into the last lock some few hundred yards before the tunnel mouth'.

continued on page 72

Route 16

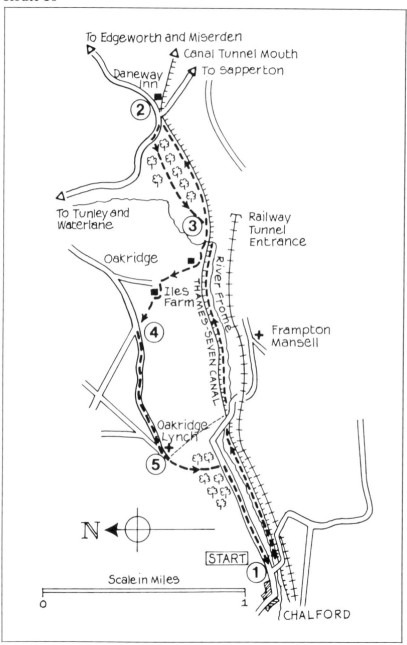

To Edgeworth and Miserden

Canal Tunnel Mouth

To Sapperton

Daneway Inn

2

To Tunley and Waterlane

Oakridge

3

Railway Tunnel Entrance

River Frome

Iles Farm

THAMES-SEVEN CANAL

4

Frampton Mansell

Oakridge Lynch

5

N

START

1

Scale in Miles

0

1

CHALFORD

Route 16

Thames – Severn Canal

6½ miles
(Variations - 5 and 8 miles)

Start

*Chalford village, on the A419 (Stroud to Cirencester road), 4 miles east of Stroud. Approaching from Stroud, watch for the Chalford Vale sign and leave the A419 by the telephone box and garage. Take a narrow road indicated 'Unsuitable for heavy goods vehicles' (i.e. straight on). Ignore left turns along this **very narrow** road and park on the verge, near a playground, in ½ mile, just beyond the junction with a road on the right crossing the canal. (O.S. Sheet Landranger 163, G.R. 904025).*

Route

1. *Walk back to the road junction and from the bridge, follow the 'Daneway and Sapperton' sign along the towpath. Keep on this bank until the obvious crossing place over a bridge near some converted cottages. Watch here for the footpath signpost. Approaching Daneway, the path reverts to the left bank over a footbridge at a lock.*

2. *From the inn, take the climbing road signposted Waterlane and Bisley. Soon, opposite a gate into a field, turn left along a woodland track into Siccarage Wood Nature Reserve. Keep to the main path as it zig-zags downhill (very muddy in patches after rain).*

3. *Descend to the canal by a bridge passed earlier. (Those wishing to avoid the climb to Oakridge can return the way they came by taking the towpath to the right here). Otherwise, turn right and ascend a stony track which is metalled beyond a cottage. Turn left at a junction to pass Iles Farm and cut a corner by crossing a stile on the left beyond a house called Greenways. The path crosses a field diagonally to the left to reach a road junction. Follow the signpost indicating Oakridge Lynch.*

4. *Keep straight on, ignoring tempting side roads and paths, including a road on the left signposted Frampton Mansell and Chalford. Go over a crossroads, passing a green and a school on the right and a church on the left. At the end of the green, follow a signposted footpath through an odd metal stile between a house and a garage. Keep first a wall, then a hedge on the left down a sloping field. After crossing 2 more stiles, skirt the right-hand edge of a wood for 40 metres before entering it through a fence. Descend a clear track to meet a road. Turn right for an easy ½ -mile walk back to the car.*

Variations

As indicated above, a shorter variation would be to retrace steps from the bridge after leaving the wood. Those wishing to see the tunnel mouth can extend the walk by keeping to the towpath for another ¾ mile beyond the Daneway Inn.

Refreshments

Daneway Inn. Bar snacks, Morning coffee. Garden. Children welcome.

Today, the old canal is a haven for wild life. Water-loving plants flourish along the banks, in the old locks and on the canal bed. Dragonflies abound, and bird life, especially along the well-wooded stretches, provides interest throughout.

Note
The restored southern entrance to the tunnel can be inspected just off the minor road between Coates and Tarlton (O.S. GR 965006).

River Windrush, Bourton-on-the-Water.

72

Useful information

Routes in Order of Difficulty

Easy short walks (less than 5 miles)
    Route   1 - Around Chipping Campden
    Route   8 - Bourton-on-the-Water lakes

More strenuous walks (less than 5 miles)
    Route   5 - High Cotswold - Cleeve Common
    Route 12 - Chedworth Woods and Roman Villa

Easy longer walks (5 or more miles)
    Route   6 - Upper Windrush Valley
    Route   7 - Three Rivers Walk
    Route   9 - Upper Coln Valley
    Route 11 - Churn Valley
    Route 13 - Around Painswick
    Route 14 - Duntisbourne and Winstone
    Route 15 - Lower Coln Valley
    Route 16 - Thames - Severn Canal (Towpath each way)

More strenuous longer walks (5 or more miles)
    Route   2 - Stanway and Stanton
    Route   3 - Hailes Abbey and Winchcombe
    Route   4 - Winchcombe and Belas Knap
    Route 10 - Wold Villages Walk
    Route 16 - Thames - Severn Canal (return via Oakridge)

Bus Operators in the Cotswold Area

Castleways (Winchcombe) Ltd., Greet Road, Winchcombe. Tel. 01242 602949.
Pulham & Sons, Station Road, Bourton-on-the-Water. Tel. 01451 820369.
Swanbrook, Staverton nr. Cheltenham. Tel. 01452 712386
Villager Community Bus, Embury Ring, Condicote, Stow-on-the-Wold. Tel. 01451 831594

Wet weather alternatives (completely or partly under cover)
Museums and art galleries

Arlington Mill Museum, Bibury. Open daily Easter to Christmas. Tel. 01285 740368.
Beatrix Potter Museum, 9 College Court, Gloucester. Open Monday to Saturday all year. Tel. 01452 422856.
Cheltenham Museum & Art Gallery, Clarence Street, Cheltenham. Open all year. Tel. 01242 237431.
City Museum & Art Gallery, Brunswick Road, Gloucester. Open all year Monday to Saturday and Sundays July to September. Tel. 01452 524131.
Corinium Museum, Park Street, Cirencester. Open all week. Tel. 01285 655611.
Cotswold Countryside Collection, The Old Prison, Northleach. Agricultural bygones and old prison. Open daily April to October. Tel. 01451 860715.
Folk Museum, Bishop Hooper's Lodgings, 99-103 Westgate Street, Gloucester. Open all year. Tel. 01452 526467.

Gustav Holst Birthplace Museum, 4 Clarence Road, Cheltenham. Open Tuesday to Saturday all year. Tel. 01242 524846.

John Moore Countryside Museum, Tewkesbury. Open Easter to October. Tel. 01684 297174.

Little Museum, 45 Church Street, Tewkesbury. Open Easter to October, Tuesday to Saturday. Tel. 01684 297174.

Motor Museum, Bourton-on-the-Water. Open February to November. Tel. 01451 821255.

Railway Museum, 23 Gloucester Street, Winchcombe. Open Easter, Bank Holidays and weekends to end of October. Tel. 01242 602257.

Railway Centre, Toddington Station, near Winchcombe. Steam train trips, weekends and Bank Holidays. Tel. 01242 621405.

Soldiers of Gloucestershire Regimental Museum, The Old Customs House, Commercial Road, Gloucester Docks. Open weekdays throughout year. Tel. 01452 522682.

Stroud & District Museum, Lansdown, Stroud. Open throughout year, Tuesdays. Tel. 01453 763394.

Town Museum, 64 Barton Street, Tewkesbury. Open daily, April to October. Tel. 01684 295027.

Winchcombe Folk and Police Museum, Old Town Hall, Winchcombe. Open Mondays to Saturdays. Tel. 01242 602925.

Woolstapler's Hall Museum, High Street, Chipping Campden. Open April to September and weekends during October. Tel. 01386 840289.

World of Mechanical Music, High Street, Northleach. Open daily. Tel. 01451 860181.

Historic Buildings Open to the public.

Chastleton House, Chastleton, near Moreton-in-Marsh. (National Trust). Jacobean Manor, Topiary Garden. Open Friday to Sunday, April to October. Tel. 01608 74355

Daneway House, Sapperton. March to October, by appointment only. Tel. 01285 760232.

Painswick Rococo Gardens. Open Wednesday to Sunday. Tel. 01452 813204.

Pittville Pump Room, Albert Road, Cheltenham. Open Wednesday to Monday. Tel. 01242 523852.

Snowshill Manor, Snowshill, near Moreton-in-Marsh. (National Trust). Open Wednesday to Sunday, April to October, and Bank Holiday Monday. Tel. 01386 852410.

Sudeley Castle, Winchcombe. Open March to October. Tel. 01242 602308.

Other Places of Interest (completely or partly under cover)

Birdland Park, Bourton-on-the-Water. Open daily. Tel. 01451 820480

Brewery Arts, Cricklade Street, Cirencester. Craft Gallery, Coffee House. Open all year. Tel. 01451 850675

Brass Rubbing Centre, The Cathedral, Gloucester. Open Monday to Saturday, July and August

Cotswold Falconry Centre, Batsford Park, Nr. Moreton-in-Marsh. Open March-Nov. Tel. 01386 701043.

Chedworth Roman Villa, (National Trust), Yanworth, near Northleach. Open March to October, Tuesday to Sunday, and Bank Holiday. Also November to mid December and February, Wednesday to Sunday. Tel. 01242 890256. (See Route 12).

Gloucestershire Wildlife Trust Headquarters, Dulverton Building, Robinswood Hill, Gloucester. Tel. 01452 383333.

Hailes Abbey (EH and National Trust), near Winchcombe. Open April to October. Not Mondays or Tuesdays during winter months. Tel. 01242 602398. (See Route 3).

Model Railway Exhibition, Bourton-on-the-Water. Open daily in school holidays and April to September. Weekends October to March. Tel. 01451 820686.

Model Village, Bourton-on-the-Water. Open all year. Tel. 01451 420467.

Prinknash Abbey Pottery & Bird Park, near Painswick. Open all year (pottery shop). Bird park Easter to October. Tel. 01452 812239

For more information

'Discover the Countryside' is Gloucestershire County Council's campaign to encourage visitors to get off the beaten track and explore the county's beautiful countryside. The campaign offers plenty of information to help families make the most of their explorations.

A wide range of free colour leaflets and factsheets is available, among them, *Walking in Gloucestershire*, which highlights countryside and town trails, long distance walks, walking holidays and a range of guided walks organised by the Cotswolds AONB Service, National Trust and Wildlife Trust. Factsheets include *Walks in the Cotswolds*, *Walks in the Forest of Dean*, *Walks in the Severn Vale*.

Cycling in Gloucestershire, and a cycling factsheet are also available. Other free factsheets include: *Arts & Crafts Attractions; Attractions Accessible by Disabled People; Attractions with Free Admission; Country Parks, Picnic Sites & Access; Farms Open to the Public; Fishing, Forestry Commission Properties, Industrial Heritage Attractions, Accommodation Information, Camping and Caravanning Guide* - and many others.

To obtain any of these free leaflets and factsheets, and to find out more about Gloucestershire and the Cotswolds, contact Gloucestershire Tourism, Environment Department, Shire Hall, Gloucester GL1 2TH. Tel. 01452 425673.

Two Outstanding Cotswold Hill Trails
1. Crickley Hill Country Park
(1¼ miles with several additional alternatives)

Summary

Crickley Hill Country Park consists of 114 acres of grassland, woodland and heavily quarried exposed rocks. Ownership is shared between the Gloucestershire County Council and the National Trust. Quarrying of the fossil-rich beds of jurassic limestone ceased in 1963 and since then archaeological excavations have revealed a fascinating story of the colonisation of the area by successive races of people since Neolithic times. There are superb views westwards to the Forest of Dean and beyond to the Welsh mountains.

Attractions

Few, if any country parks can offer such a wealth of interest to both young and old as Crickley Hill. The route described overleaf is intended to show something of the ancient history of the site, as revealed by the archaeological digs which take place every summer. However, a geological walk, examining the quarries and searching for fossils, in the oolitic and pea-grit limestone rocks, can be equally rewarding. While for nature lovers, the beechwoods and open grassland are rich in wild life, providing a range of flowers, butterflies and birds, together with fungi in the autumn. In fact a whole day could well be spent following the different trails or alternatively, several visits made at varying times of the year.

Start

Park car park, reached by access road from B4070 near its junction with the A436 and A417 at the roundabout near the Air Balloon Inn, 4 miles south of Cheltenham. (O.S. Sheet 163, GR 930163).

Route

Archaeological trail from the Information Office, from which detailed Hill Fort trail leaflet can be obtained. Follow the dark brown-topped posts.

2. Leckhampton Hill (1¼ miles with several additional alternatives)

Summary

This fine hill, standing out impressively above Cheltenham, has been quarried for centuries, and its stone, a cream-coloured oolitic limestone known as freestone, can be seen in such buildings as Shire Hall, Gloucester, Cheltenham College Chapel and Leckhampton church. Quarrying finally came to an end in 1926 and soon afterwards, the hill was bought by Cheltenham Corporation as an amenity for the town. The walk described takes in the natural history, geology and industrial history of the hill, and offers something of interest for all the family. The route is very steep in places and strong footwear is recommended.

Attractions

Cheltenham folk are justifiably proud of their local hill and when, in 1906, a landowner tried to deprive them of access to it, he literally caused a riot! The cottage which once stood on the site of the present Tramway Cottage, near the car park and now the home of the hill's custodian, was burned down by rioters and the landlord's bailiff forced to flee for his life. Today, the hill is a mecca for geologists, who come to admire the fine exposures of freestone and pea grit, so called because of the pea-size nodules found in the lower layers. Those wishing to search for fossils in the old quarries, are warned not to approach too near to the cliffs in case of rock falls.

The Devil's Chimney is an impressive sight. It is a column of rock left behind by 18th-century quarrymen and was once a great attraction to climbers. Nowadays it is carefully preserved. A search of the hill reveals remains of the old tramways - wooden and stone sleepers. The hollow shells of the quarry buildings serve as a ready-made adventure playground, but care should be taken, as before, of falling rocks.

The hill is a rewarding hunting ground for the young botanist. Jackdaws and stock doves nest in the quarry faces.

Refreshments

The Air Balloon Inn, near Crickley Hill. Morning coffee. Lunches. Children welcome.

Start

Car park on Daisy Bank Road, Leckhampton, on left hand side of B4070 (steep hill), a mile south of Cheltenham. (O.S. Sheet 163, GR 949189).

Route

As with the Crickley Hill walk, the route followed consists of 8 stops, indicated in this case by stone markers inscribed 'Leckhampton Hill Walk'.

Alternative walks

There are several other interesting walks in the locality.

Other Parks, Trails & Viewpoints

Barrow Wake viewpoint, between Crickley Hill and Birdlip. Geological dial and topograph. Open all year. Tel. 01452 425675

Batsford Park Arboretum, Batsford, near Moreton-in-Marsh. Open daily, April to October. Tel. 01608 650722.

Broadway Tower Country Park and natural history centre, Fish Hill, Broadway. Open daily April to October. Picnic site. Tel. 01386 852390.

Cooper's Hill nature trail, near Cranham. Open all year. Tel. 01452 425675

Cotswold Farm Park and trail, Bemborough Farm, near Guiting Power. Open May to September. Tel. 01451 850307.

Dover's Hill, near Chipping Campden. Viewpoint with topograph. Open all year. (See Route 1). Tel. 01684 850051

Folly Farm, near Bourton-on-the-Water. Rare breeds of poultry. Open all year. Tel. 01451 820285.

Keynes Country Park, near Cirencester. Nature walk, picnic site, playground. Part of Cotswold Water Park. Open all year. Tel. 01285 861459. (Ranger).

Kilkenny viewpoint, near Andoversford. Open all year. Tel. 01452 425675

Pittville Park, Cheltenham. Open all year. Wednesday to Monday. Tel. 01242 523852.

Sandford Park, Cheltenham. Open all year.

Pubs and Inns catering for Families

Below is a list of some of the pubs and inns in the area covered by this guide, the licensees of which make provision for families with young children. To locate them, refer to the map at the beginning of the guide.

Brockhampton — Craven Arms	**Crickley Hill** — Air Balloon Inn.
Chedworth — Seven Tuns	**Elkstone** — Highwayman Inn, Beechpike.
Cleeve Hill — High Roost	**Guiting Power** — Farmer's Arms.
Cleeve Hill — Rising Sun	**Kineton** — Half Way House.
Cold Aston — Plough Inn	**Sapperton** — Daneway Inn.
Coln St Aldwyns — New Inn	**Stanton** — Mount Inn.
Cranham — Royal William Inn.	

All the information given here was correct on publication, but times of opening, etc. are sometimes altered at short notice, so please check before setting off on a grand expedition!

THE FAMILY WALKS SERIES

Family Walks on Anglesey. Laurence Main	ISBN 0 907758 66 5
Family Walks around Bakewell & Castleton. Norman Taylor	ISBN 0 907758 37 1
Family Walks in Berkshire & North Hampshire. Kathy Sharp	ISBN 0 907758 37 1
Family Walks around Bristol, Bath & the Mendips. Nigel Vile	ISBN 0 907758 19 3
Family Walks around Cardiff & the Valleys. Gordon Hindess	ISBN 0 907758 54 1
Family Walks in the Cotswolds. Gordon Ottewell	ISBN 0 907758 15 0
Family Walks in the Dark Peak. Norman Taylor	ISBN 0 907758 16 9
Family Walks in Dorset. Nigel Vile	ISBN 0 907758 86 X
Family Walks in East Sussex. Sally & Clive Cutter	ISBN 0 907758 71 1
Family Walks on Exmoor & the Quantocks. John Caswell	ISBN 0 907758 46 0
Family Walks in Gower. Amanda Green	ISBN 0 907758 63 0
Family Walks in Gwent. Gordon Hindess	ISBN 0 907758 63 0
Family Walks in Hereford & Worcester. Gordon Ottewell	ISBN 0 907758 20 7
Family Walks on the Isle of Wight. Laurence Main	ISBN 0 907758 56 8
Family Walks around Keswick and Northern Lakeland. Timothy and Sylvia Bunker	ISBN 0 907758 93 2
Family Walks in the Lake District. Barry McKay	ISBN 0 907758 40 1
Family Walks in Leicestershire. Meg Williams	ISBN 0 907758 82 7
Family Walks in Lincolnshire. Camilla Harrison	ISBN 0 907758 67 3
Family Walks in Mendip, Avalon & Sedgemoor. Nigel Vile	ISBN 0 907758 41 X
Family Walks in Mid Wales. Laurence Main	ISBN 0 907758 27 4
Family Walks in the New Forest. Nigel Vile	ISBN 0 907758 60 6
Family Walks on the Norfolk Broads. Norman Taylor	ISBN 0 907758 90 8
Family Walks in Northamptonshire. Gordon Ottewell	ISBN 0 907758 81 9
Family Walks in the North Wales Borderlands. Gordon Emery	ISBN 0 907758 50 9
Family Walks on the North Wales Coast. Gordon Emery	ISBN 0 907758 89 4
Family Walks in North West Kent. Clive Cutter	ISBN 0 907758 36 3
Family Walks in the North Yorkshire Dales. Howard Beck	ISBN 0 907758 52 5
Family Walks in Oxfordshire. Laurence Main	ISBN 0 907758 38 X
Family Walks in Pembrokeshire. Laurence Main	ISBN 0 907758 75 4
Family Walks in Snowdonia. Laurence Main	ISBN 0 907758 32 0
Family Walks in South Derbyshire. Gordon Ottewell	ISBN 0 907758 61 4
Family Walks in South Shropshire. Marian Newton	ISBN 0 907758 30 4
Family Walks in South Yorkshire. Norman Taylor	ISBN 0 907758 25 8
Family Walks in the Staffordshire Peak & Potteries. Les Lumsdon	ISBN 0 907758 34 7
Family Walks around Stratford & Banbury. Gordon Ottewell	ISBN 0 907758 49 5
Family Walks in Suffolk. C J Francis	ISBN 0 907758 64 9
Family Walks in Surrey. Norman Bonney	ISBN 0 907758 74 6
Family Walks around Swansea. Raymond Humphreys	ISBN 0 907758 62 2
Family Walks in the Teme Valley. Camilla Harrison	ISBN 0 907758 45 2
Family Walks in Three Peaks & Malham. Howard Beck	ISBN 0 907758 42 8
Family Walks in the Weald of Kent & Sussex. Clive Cutter	ISBN 0 907758 51 7
Family Walks in West London. Caroline Bacon	ISBN 0 907758 72 X
Family Walks in West Sussex. Nick Channer	ISBN 0 907758 73 8
Family Walks in West Yorkshire. Howard Beck	ISBN 0 907758 43 6
Family Walks in the White Peak. Norman Taylor	ISBN 0 907758 09 6
More Family Walks in the White Peak. Norman Taylor	ISBN 0 907758 80 0
Family Walks in Wiltshire. Nigel Vile	ISBN 0 907758 21 5
Family Walks in the Wye Valley. Heather & John Hurley	ISBN 0 907758 26 6
Family Walks in Birmingham & West Midlands	ISBN 0 907758 83 5

If you have written a definitive book of regional interest, we may be interested in publishing it - please write or send a synopsis.

Scarthin Books of Cromford, in the Peak District, are also leading second-hand and antiquarian booksellers, and are eager to purchase specialised material, both ancient and modern. Contact Dr. D. J. Mitchell, 01629 823272